Gathering the people, settling the land

The Archaeology of a middle Thames landscape:
Anglo-Saxon to post-medieval

By Stuart Foreman, Jonathan Hiller and David Petts

with contributions by

*Carol Allen, Leigh Allen, Tim Allen, Janet Ambers, Elizabeth Anderson, Paul Backhouse,
Alistair Barclay, Paul Blinkhorn, Angela Boyle, Kayt Brown, Philip Catherall, Dawn Chambers,
Anne-Marie Cromarty, Cecily Cropper, Peter Hacking, Alan Hardy, Jill Hind, Martin Hodson,
Nigel Jeffries, Lyn Keyes, Richard Macphail, Peter Marshall, Nick Mitchell, Simon Mortimer,
Julian Munby, Ian Riddler, Adrian Parker, Daniel Poore. Adrienne Powell, Ruth Pelling,
Mark Robinson, Fiona Roe, Claire Sampson, Ian Scott, Edmund Simons*

Illustrations by
Luke Adams, Peter Lorimer, Mike Middleton, Robert Read, Ros Smith

Oxford Archaeology

Thames Valley Landscapes Monograph No. 14

The publication of this volume has been funded by the Environment Agency and Eton College

Published by Oxford Archaeology as part of the Thames Valley Landscapes Monograph series

Designed by Elizabeth Anderson, Paul Backhouse, Alan Hardy and Alistair Barclay

Edited by Alan Hardy

This book is available direct from
Oxbow Books, Park End Place, Oxford, OX1 1HN
(Phone: 01865-241249; Fax: 01865-794449)
and
The David Brown Book Company
PO Box 511, Oakville CT 06779, USA
(Phone: 860-945-9329; Fax: 860-945-9468)
or from our website
www.oxbowbooks.com

Figures 1.1-3, 2.1-4 and Plate 1.1 are reproduced from the Ordnance Survey on behalf of the controller of Her Majesty's Stationery Office, © Crown Copyright, AL 100005569

ISBN 0-904220-31-1

Typeset and printed in Europe by The Alden Group, Oxford, UK

Contents

Figures

Plates

Tables

Preface

By Alistair Barclay and Alan Hardy

This volume presents the results from the Maidenhead, Windsor and Eton Flood Alleviation Scheme (Environment Agency) and the Eton College Rowing Course Project. The two projects contained within a 12 km stretch of the middle Thames valley, provide two contrasting windows onto a landscape. During the fieldwork and assessment stages they were undertaken as two independent projects and because of their complementary evidence it was decided to publish the results as a series of three monographs. This monograph, *Gathering the people, settling the land*, covers the period from post-Roman times, while two further volumes, *Opening the wood, making the land*, and *Bridging the river, dividing the land* will cover the Mesolithic to earlier Bronze Age and later Bronze Age to Roman periods, respectively.

Both projects contribute much new evidence towards the understanding of a landscape history, although it is acknowledged that the coverage is uneven and incomplete. However, the combined results do provide a considerable body of evidence for the basis of a narrative on one particular middle Thames landscape, which in time can be re-evaluated as new evidence comes to light.

This volume covers aspects of the post-Roman landscape, in particular the identification of an extensive middle Saxon site of unusual character — a site that is composed entirely of pits and one that cannot be easily placed into an identifiable category of Saxon settlement. There is evidence for consumption of goods more typical of urban centres, with little sign of production or permanent settlement. Because of its peculiar character we felt it necessary to make as much of the site archive available to the reader as possible.

In designing these volumes it was recognised that the two projects had produced a significant quantity of data, and that this lent itself to an alternative approach to publication. The format of this report takes the form of a printed synthesis accompanied by a CD-ROM that contains additional information and data supporting the printed text, and a selective digital archive, a major part of which is interactive. Not every reader will have access to a computer so the intention is that the printed text can be read and understood as a stand-alone publication, while the CD-ROM holds more detailed specialist and contextual data. A printed copy of the CD-ROM is available as part of the publication archive held by Buckingham County Museum, Reading Museum and as fiche at the National Monument Record Office, Swindon and at Oxford Archaeology's Archive Department.

Introduction to the CD-ROM

By Elizabeth Anderson and Paul Backhouse

The CD-ROM is split into three main sections:

- Project background and local area information
- Site specific information including detailed Anglo-Saxon pit information
- Specialist Reports.

The first section of the CD-ROM serves to place the project in its wider context with articles on historic background, relevance to the surrounding area and project research designs. The user will also be able to consult a full digital version of the monograph,

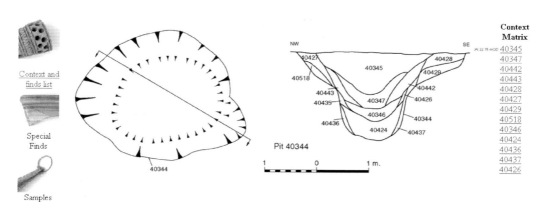

Context and finds list

Special Finds

Samples

Photographic record

Plan and section

Pit 40344. The pit was circular with a concave profile. It was 1.82 m deep and had a diameter of 2.84 m. The basal fill was a silty sand (40436 = 40437), overlain by a yellow-brown sandy silt (40424) that contained prehistoric and Roman pottery and animal bone. Above lay a yellow-grey sandy silt (40346) with pottery and animal bone, in turn sealed by grey-brown silty sand (40442 = 40443). Above this a yellow-brown sandy silt (40347) was deposited, containing one Iron Age sherd, one Roman tile fragment and animal bone. The final fill was yellow-brown silty sand (40345) containing nine sherds of early-middle Saxon pottery, two sherds of Roman pottery and animal bone. Charred seed and chaff were present in context 40345 and 40424 together with free-threshing cereal grain; weed seeds were common, as was charcoal (ss nos 40023-25).

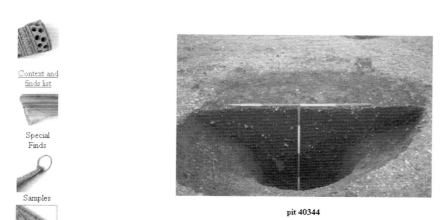

Context and finds list

Special Finds

Samples

Photographic record

Plan and section

pit 40344

Pit 40344. The pit was circular with a concave profile. It was 1.82 m deep and had a diameter of 2.84 m. The basal fill was a silty sand (40436 = 40437), overlain by a yellow-brown sandy silt (40424) that contained prehistoric and Roman pottery and animal bone. Above lay a yellow-grey sandy silt (40346) with pottery and animal bone, in turn sealed by grey-brown silty sand (40442 = 40443). Above this a yellow-brown sandy silt (40347) was deposited, containing one Iron Age sherd, one Roman tile fragment and animal bone. The final fill was yellow-brown silty sand (40345) containing nine sherds of early-middle Saxon pottery, two sherds of Roman pottery and animal bone. Charred seed and chaff were present in context 40345 and 40424 together with free-threshing cereal grain; weed seeds were common, as was charcoal (ss nos 40023-25).

available to download as a PDF file. A digital bibliography is also available. To a certain extent this section reflects what is also available in the traditional printed media.

The second part of the CD-ROM, which is accessed through the use of interactive maps, contains site specific information. Using a toolbar, the user will be able to zoom in and around the map itself. The same toolbar also allows the user to view the main phases of Lake End Road West, Lot's Hole and Lake End Road East. The distributions of certain artefacts such as bone combs and pottery will also be available for Lake End Road West. Clicking on a single pit on any of these plans will launch an individual page, which holds information concerning the feature. Finds information (including weight or sherd number where appropriate) and illustrations, environmental analysis and radiocarbon dating are available where applicable by clicking on the appropriate icons on the toolbar.

The final section contains the specialist reports, which can be accessed either through the individual pit pages, or through the home page. These reports hold the more detailed finds information and tables.

Instructions

Insert the CD-ROM into drive. It should automatically run, if it does not press the start button and select the run option.

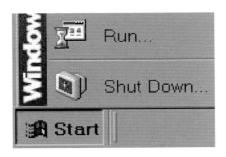

A dialog appears. Type in the name of your CD-ROM drive, which will probably be D: followed by \envag.exe. So for example type D:\envag.exe and click OK.

Technical details of the CD-ROM

The CD-ROM was written using Html, Flash and Java to allow for cross-platform compatibility, as well as allowing the user to extract the data to a multitude of programs. All programs needed to run the bulk of the CD-ROM will be available to be installed from the CD-ROM.

Minimum Specification: – Pentium 200mhz, 32mb Ram 100mb of hard drive space. Windows 95 and Internet explorer 5.0.

Preferred Specification: – Pentium 400mhz, 64mb Ram 100mb of hard drive space. Windows 95 and Microsoft Internet explorer 5.0.

The CD-ROM is best viewed in 800 × 600 pixels, using Internet Explorer.

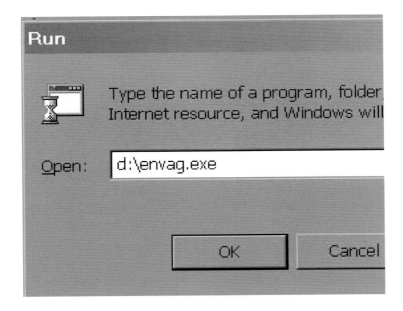

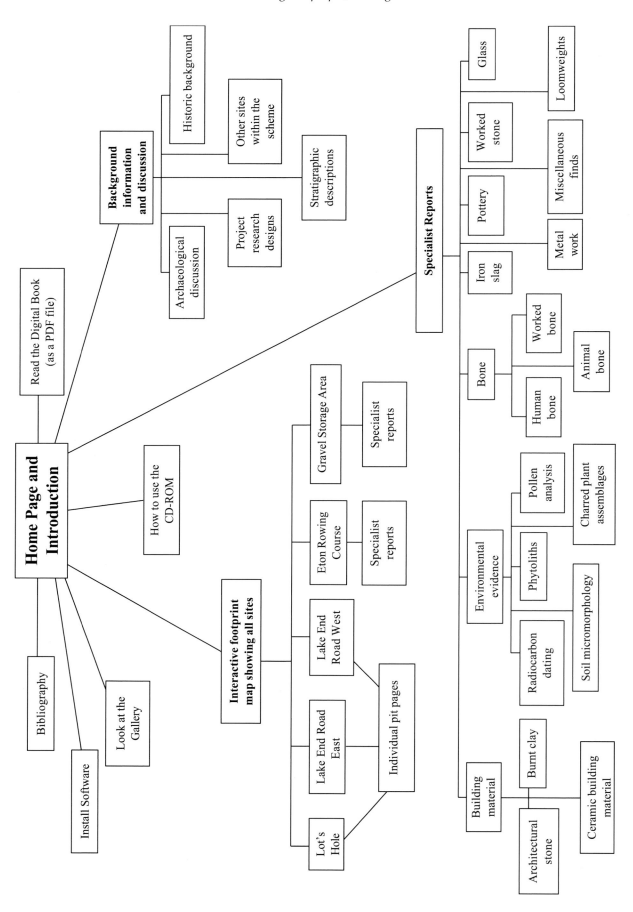

Acknowledgements

The Maidenhead, Windsor and Eton Flood Alleviation Scheme

The excavations and post-excavation programme were funded entirely by the Environment Agency (EA). Throughout the project Oxford Archaeology (OA formerly Oxford Archaeological Unit (OAU)) has received support and encouragement from Phil Catherall, the EA Archaeologist. The fieldwork programme was initially coordinated by George Lambrick (formerly of OA) and subsequently by Mark Roberts. The Phase 1 excavations at Lot's Hole and Lake End Road East were undertaken by Mark Roberts and Jonathan Hunn respectively. The Phase 1 post-excavation assessment and research design was coordinated by Tess Durden and Mark Roberts. Preliminary post-excavation analysis was undertaken by Simon Mortimer, Neil McNabb and Dan Poore. The Phase 2 excavation at Lake End Road West was undertaken by Stuart Foreman who also coordinated the Phase 2 post-excavation assessment and the revised research design. The overall post-excavation programme was initially coordinated by Philippa Bradley and then by Alistair Barclay. The post-excavation programme was initially managed by Stuart Foreman and Jon Hiller and assisted by Anne-Marie Cromarty and Elizabeth Anderson. Alan Hardy and Alistair Barclay are responsible for the book design, while Elizabeth Anderson and Paul Backhouse designed and compiled the CD-ROM. Illustrations were coordinated by Luke Adams and undertaken by Rob Read and Mike Middleton. The cover design is by Peter Lorimer. We would also like to thank the many excavators and the support of our many colleagues at OA, in particular Leigh Allen, Alison Gledhill, Greg Campbell and Dana Challinor for organising the finds and environmental research programmes.

During the post-excavation programme the project team has benefited from discussions with many individuals, in particular Tim Allen, Anne Dodd, Dr Helena Hamerow, Dr John Blair, Phil Catherall, Maria Walters and David Hinton who acted as academic referee. We would also like to thank Peter Marshall (English Heritage) and Janet Ambers (British Museum) for their assistance with the radiocarbon dating programme. We would also like to thank Mike Farley (former Buckinghamshire County Archaeologist) and Alexander (Sandy) Kidd (Buckinghamshire Environmental Services Senior Archaeological Officer).

Julian Munby would like to acknowledge the assistance of Jill Hind, Mrs Peregrine Palmer and Penny Hatfield, Archivist of Eton College. For the Saxon part of the animal bone report, Adrienne Powell would like to thank Keith Dobney for sharing unpublished data from Flixborough. For the medieval part of the animal bone report, Kate Clark examined the dog specimen and the pathological material and Alison Locker identified the fish bone. Richard Macphail would like to thank Greg Campbell and Stuart Foreman for their collaboration. Thin-section manufacture was by Spectrum Petrographics, Oregon and chemical analyses by the Laboratory for Environmental Archaeology, Department of Archaeology, Umeå University, is also acknowledged.

Lot's Hole Gravel Storage Area

The project was funded by Summerleaze Ltd and the archaeological work was managed by Stuart Foreman and the fieldwork was undertaken by Granville Laws. Additional work was also undertaken by W S Atkins and managed by Dr Jim Wilson. The post-excavation analysis was undertaken by Anne-Marie Cromarty. Additional support and advice was given by Phil Catherall (EA). We would also like to thank W Kirkpatrick (Director, Summerleaze Ltd) and Alexander (Sandy) Kidd (Buckinghamshire Environmental Services Senior Archaeological Officer).

The Eton College Rowing Course Project

The excavations and post-excavation analysis relevant to this volume were entirely funded by Eton College. The support of Roderick Watson, Special Projects Advisor to the College, and of Brian Duckett, who has dealt with archaeological matters on his behalf, is gratefully acknowledged. The excavations were carried out under the direction of Tim Allen and Ken Welsh of the OAU, who would like to thank the professional staff of OAU who assisted, and the many volunteers who worked on the site. The project has been fortunate to have an Archaeological Liaison Committee chaired by James Graham-Campbell that has overseen progress, and we would like to thank all of its members for their support and advice. We are also grateful to Mike Farley, Julia Wise and Sandy Kidd of Buckinghamshire County Council for their guidance throughout the project.

Tim Allen would like to thank all of the contributors to the sections of the publication dealing with the Eton Rowing Course, and Anne-Marie Cromarty, Nick Mitchell and David Petts for their assistance with the phasing of the post-Roman deposits and the archaeological description. Janet Ambers at the British Museum radiocarbon dating facility is gratefully acknowledged for her assistance. The drawing of the Saxon burial was carried out by Mike Middleton.

Location of the project archives

The archive of the Eton Rowing Course Project is deposited with Buckinghamshire County Museum. The archive of the Flood Alleviation Scheme is split between Buckinghamshire County Museum and Berkshire Museum, Reading. A copy of the archive will also be deposited with the National Monuments Record Centre, Swindon.

Chapter 1: Introduction

by Jonathan Hiller, David Petts, Stuart Foreman and Tim Allen

SUMMARY
by David Petts

The excavations by Oxford Archaeology (formerly Oxford Archaeological Unit) on the sites of the Environment Agency's Maidenhead, Windsor and Eton Flood Alleviation Scheme and the Eton College Rowing Course adjacent to the river Thames in Buckinghamshire and Berkshire have given archaeologists an unprecedented opportunity to examine a landscape within the middle Thames valley (Fig. 1.1).

The Anglo-Saxon and medieval archaeology of the middle Thames valley is not as well understood as the region of the upper Thames to the west of the Chilterns or London and the Thames Estuary to the east (Fig. 1.1). However, the high status mid 7th century furnished barrow burial at Taplow and the excavated, but unpublished, palace site at Old Windsor clearly indicate the importance of this area.

During the Saxon period the Thames functioned both as a border and a communication route. Navigable for most of its course, it served to bring both people and traded goods from the south-east of the country into the heart of central southern England. Once *Lundenwic* was established as the foremost trading site in Anglo-Saxon England this aspect of the river's use became even more important.

However, the Thames Valley also served as a major political boundary. While it is difficult to reconstruct the early Anglo-Saxon political history of the area it is clear that in the middle Saxon period the Thames was an important and contested border between the powerful kingdoms of Wessex and Mercia. The monastery at Cookham, only a few kilometres upriver, was for a long time a bone of contention between the rulers of the two kingdoms. In a slightly later period, the presence of a series of burghal forts along the river demonstrates the strategic position the Thames held in the 9th/10th centuries.

While archaeological discoveries and historical research have illuminated our understanding of the upper Thames to the west and the lower Thames and the estuary to the east, the nature of Saxon settlement in the period in the middle Thames valley, particularly north of the river, has remained elusive and obscure. Was there really no major Saxon settlement there? With no apparent evidence of any major Saxon or early medieval settlement focus, how did this area relate to the important sites at Taplow, upriver, or Windsor downriver? Was the area merely uninhabited pastureland? Given the political importance of the Thames as a border between Mercia and Wessex through much of the Saxon period, was this an area in dispute, and if so, is this reflected in the remains (or lack of them) to be found.

With no focus to provide a research target, the only way to get close to any overall understanding of such a large area would be through fieldwork on a large-scale – both non-intrusive (fieldwalking) and intrusive (excavation). Field evaluation along the route of the Flood Alleviation Scheme recognised what at first was considered to be extensive Saxon settlement, while subsequent excavation revealed the true extent and character of this activity.

In the event the results of the two projects have produced an exceptional site of Anglo-Saxon date, suggesting occupation and activity unlike that from any existing 'type site'. Its unique nature is perhaps best seen as a product of the role that the middle Thames valley played, as both axis and boundary, in the middle Saxon period. Exotic finds hint at wealth and high status, trade contacts with London and other parts of middle Saxon England and identify this as no ordinary site. Why did people gather at the site of a long abandoned Roman farmstead not far from the river Thames; what was their purpose and where did they come from?

THE PROJECTS
by Jonathan Hiller and Tim Allen

The two projects, the Maidenhead, Windsor and Eton Flood Alleviation Scheme (Environment Agency) and the Eton College Rowing Course Project, are contained within a 12 km stretch of the middle Thames valley (Fig. 1.2). The difference in the designs of the projects – one a linear scheme approximately 12 km long and the other contained within a defined project area measuring 3 by 1 km – provide two contrasting windows onto a landscape.

The Maidenhead, Windsor and Eton Flood Alleviation Scheme
by Jonathan Hiller

After some years of initial study, in March 1989 Thames Water published its proposals for the new flood alleviation channel. The agreed archaeological mitigation strategy was for three stages of work. Stage 1 comprised a preliminary study of the archaeological implications of the Flood Alleviation Scheme, undertaken by Buckinghamshire County Museum (Hunn *et al.*, 1990). Stage 2 consisted of a fieldwalking programme supplemented by a small amount of geophysical survey along the proposed channel route. Cropmarks were also identified and interpreted as possible monuments and enclosures. Stage 3 consisted of an archaeological field evaluation along the proposed channel route, carried out by Thames Valley Archaeological Services (TVAS) in

1

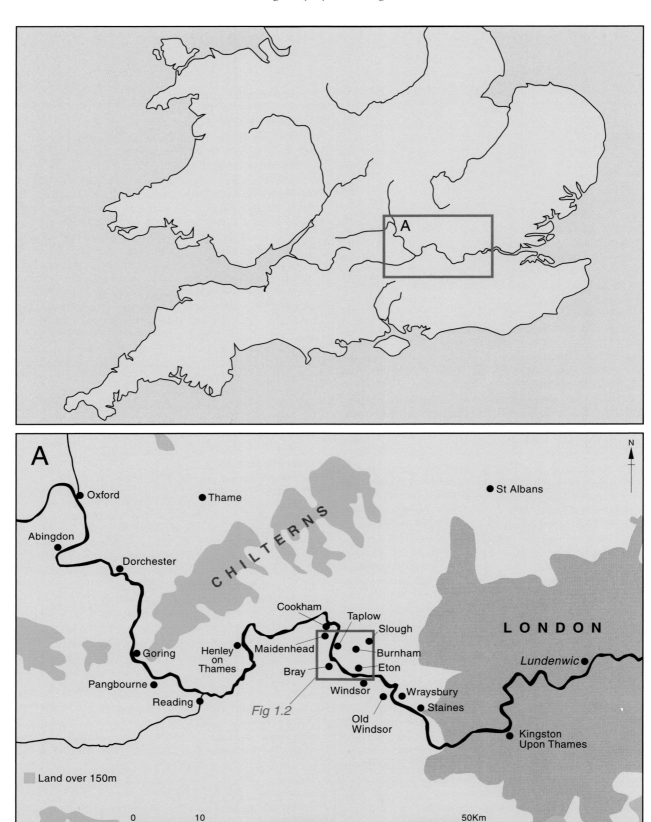

Figure 1.1   *General site location, including places identified in the text*

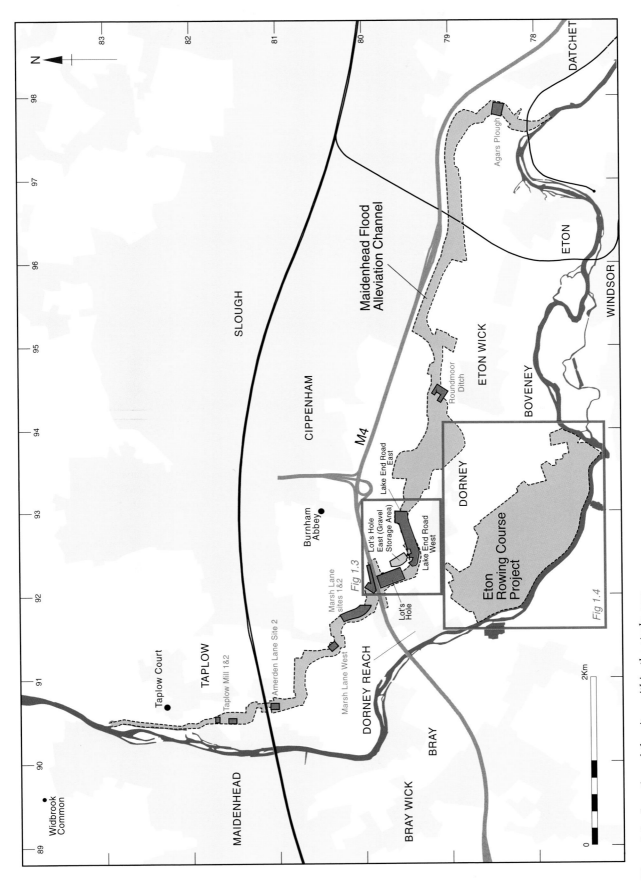

Figure 1.2 Location of the sites within the study area

1991. The fieldwork consisted of 993 evaluation trenches, excavated between January and March of that year (Ford 1991). The trenching was supplemented by augering and test pits.

As a result of this work, both Buckinghamshire and Berkshire County Councils attached an archaeological condition to the proposed channel scheme. In response, the then National Rivers Authority (NRA) commissioned Oxford Archaeological Unit (OAU) to undertake a programme of fieldwork to preserve by record the archaeology along the route.

Two seasons of excavation (see Fig. 1.3 and Pl. 1.1) were undertaken in 1996 and 1997 under the overall direction of George Lambrick (OAU 1997, 1998), to the north of the village of Dorney. The 1996 excavations at Lake End Road East were supervised by Jonathan Hunn; in the same year Mark Roberts managed the excavation at Lot's Hole. In 1997 Stuart Foreman undertook the extensive excavations at Lake End Road West, and acted as project manager.

From 1996 to 1998 the excavations were augmented by a watching brief on the remainder of the topsoil stripping of the scheme conducted by Philip Catherall of the Environment Agency. In 1999 a watching brief was conducted by OAU on behalf of

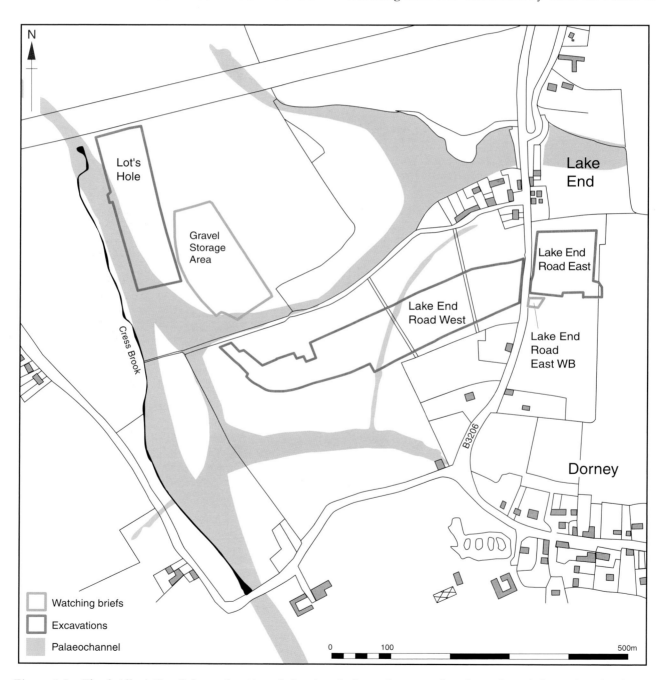

Figure 1.3 *Flood Alleviation Scheme: location of sites in relation to known palaeochannels and the modern landscape*

Plate 1.1   *Aerial photograph of Dorney and the area around Lake End, showing the palaeochannels, silted hollows and some of the Anglo-Saxon pits. Ordnance Survey © Crown Copyright OS/70271*

Summerleaze Ltd during the construction of a gravel storage area immediately east of Lot's Hole.

Other sites on the route of the Flood Alleviation Scheme that revealed post-Roman archaeology are detailed in a section of the CD-ROM.

The Eton College Rowing Course Project
by Tim Allen

When Eton College took the decision in 1985 to provide a rowing course for their pupils on land at Dorney Reach, the then Thames Water Authority (TWA – now the Environment Agency) were already considering a flood relief channel, and for some time both they and Eton College investigated the possibility of a joint Rowing Course and Flood Alleviation Channel. Thames Water commissioned a cropmark and fieldwalking survey of the Dorney area (Pl. 1.1), which was carried out by Buckinghamshire County Museum. This was completed in March 1986 (Carstairs 1986a), and a summary was published (Carstairs 1986b).

Between 1987 and 1993 a 0.5% sample of the 75 hectares under threat was evaluated, and in 1994 and 1995 a further 200 trenches averaging 30 m in length were excavated, comprising a 2% sample of the threatened part of the site.

By 1993 the different needs of the Rowing Course and the Flood Alleviation Channel had led to the separation of the two projects, and the proposed Rowing Course was no longer linked to the Thames. Eton College subsequently appointed an Archaeological Liaison Committee to advise on the appropriate research objectives and excavation strategy early in 1995.

Area excavations in the following three years were staffed by a professional team from OAU, supported by a larger number of volunteers drawn from British and overseas universities, local societies and other interested amateurs. Further excavations in 2000 were largely staffed by professionals.

An archaeological mitigation strategy was agreed between Buckinghamshire County Council and Eton College in June 1996, and was approved by the County Archaeologist, Mike Farley. The aim of the strategy was to understand the development of the landscape and human involvement within it, and three aspects of the archaeology were targeted for specific investigation: the former Thames channel, the alluvial floodplain and the cropmark gravel terrace sites. The location of the excavated sites along with those areas covered by the phases of watching brief is shown on Figure 1.4.

Minimal medieval activity was found during the evaluations, and Saxon activity was restricted to a single burial. Consequently the contribution of the Eton College Rowing Course Archaeological Project to this volume is limited. For this reason, details of the evaluation and excavation methodology are not described here, and will be detailed in the monographs devoted to the prehistoric and Roman archaeology. The use of the site during the post-Roman period is discussed in the general topographic survey of the medieval landscape.

Flood Alleviation Scheme excavation methodology
by Stuart Foreman

The excavation methodology for the Flood Alleviation Scheme is described below, while details of the

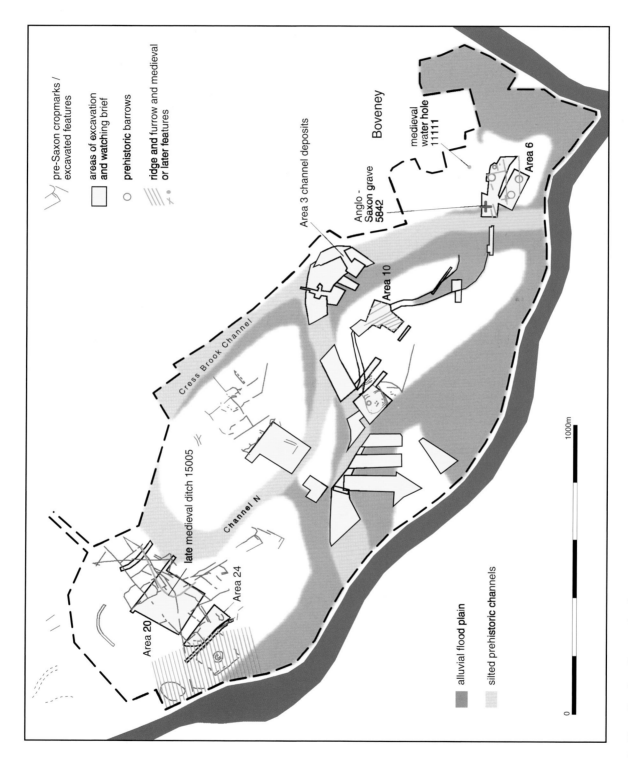

Figure 1.4 Eton Rowing Course development area: excavation and watching brief areas and principal Saxon and medieval features

Eton Rowing Course Project can be found in the monographs dealing with the prehistoric and Roman periods.

Within the umbrella of the Flood Alleviation Scheme there were variations in the methodological approach; the evaluation results for each site were reassessed once stripping was completed, and the revealed archaeology was selectively excavated in the light of the defined research priorities. So for instance, at both Lot's Hole and Lake End Road East priority was given to the investigation of the Anglo-Saxon features and discrete medieval features such as pits and the posthole buildings. Investigation of linear features away from the settlement focus was not accorded a high priority. Post-Roman archaeology, with which this report is concerned was present on three excavations and two supplementary watching briefs and their methodologies are outlined below.

The first phase of work encompassed the excavations at Lot's Hole (DLH 96) and Lake End Road East (DOLER 96) (see Fig. 1.3). The excavation of the intervening site, Lake End Road West (LERW 97) took place the following year. The watching brief on the Gravel Storage Area at Lot's Hole East (DLOTH 99) took place in 1999 and in the same year a small area to the south of Lake End Road East was also subject to a watching brief (Fig. 1.3).

Lake End Road East, Lot's Hole and Lake End Road West

The location of all three sites is shown on Figure 1.3, in relation to palaeochannels and the modern landscape. In the case of all three excavations, the overburden, consisting of topsoil and sporadic relict ploughsoil, was stripped by a mechanical excavator equipped with a toothless ditching bucket (see Pl. 1.2) Depending on the underlying drift geology, this action exposed either fairly clean flinty gravel or overlying silty clay alluvium, into which were cut negative features, principally pits, postholes and ditches.

Prehistoric and Roman features were found in parts of the excavation areas; these features and their finds are detailed in the corresponding volumes: *Opening the wood, making the land, and Bridging the river, dividing the land*. The effect that the earlier archaeology may have had on the later developments on the sites is discussed at greater length in Chapter 5.

All features were recorded in plan, but the degree to which these features were investigated by excavation varied according to their research priority. Initial spot dating of features allowed a provisional separation of features into two groups – Anglo-Saxon and medieval/post-medieval.

Excavation method and sampling policy

Anglo-Saxon pits

Pits at all of the sites were initially half-sectioned. A comparatively small number of pits were found and excavated at Lake End Road East and Lot'sHole, with limited potential for an environmental strategy: sufficient samples were taken to characterise the pit fills and identify variation within individual pit fill sequences. At Lake End Road West, after an initial assessment of the potential of the finds and environmental evidence and discussions with the County Archaeologist and The Environment Agency, it was decided to excavate the second halves of many of the

Plate 1.2 *Lake End Road West stripping the topsoil*

pits, to maximise the data retrieved. This resulted in the second halves of 34 Saxon pits being excavated, including 32 of those selected for environmental sampling.

Sampling strategy

A programme of soil-sampling was implemented, in which a total of *c* 4813 litres of deposits were recovered from 80 Saxon contexts (38 individual pit features). Aside from samples collected for initial assessment purposes, the standard soil sample size was 80 litres (or 100% of the deposit, if less than 80 litres was present).

A detailed study was undertaken on seven of the Saxon pits (comprising approximately a 10% sample of the Lake End Road West pits), and a more general comparative study of a further 31 pits (a 50% sample of the Lake End Road West pits). Pits were selected for sampling initially by classifying them according to simple size and profile characteristics, without sampling those intercutting with non-Saxon features to reduce the risk of contamination. The samples were distributed evenly between the profile classes and spatially across the site, until the predetermined percentage sample was reached. Within these limits, the most artefact-rich features and contexts were preferred for sampling.

In the case of the pits selected for detailed study, samples were taken from each fill identified, excluding some minor weathering deposits. Soil micromorphological samples were also taken from the primary, secondary and tertiary fills of two of the pits sampled in detail (40422 and 41266). For the purpose of the wider study, from each selected pit fills 1–3 were sampled. These fills were usually the richest in artefacts or animal bones. The majority of samples were 'whole soil', that is with no finds removed (except fragile small finds, which were recorded in three dimensions before removal). Most of the samples were collected following excavation and recording of the first half of the pit, by taking soil from the exposed section.

Medieval/post-medieval

Virtually all of the significant medieval and post-medieval archaeology was found in the Lot's Hole and Lake End Road East sites. In each case, all features were planned after initial cleaning. The evaluation had indicated probable nuclei of activity and/or occupation, and excavation was concentrated – in these areas – primarily on pits, intersections of the major enclosure ditches, and concentrations of postholes.

Bulk sampling was undertaken on fills within some of the medieval pits which showed visible evidence of environmental potential.

Phasing

Inevitably, the selective excavation policy, allied to the scarcity of stratigraphic relationships and the predominance of discrete features has caused difficulties with the phasing of the sites. This is exacerbated by the lack of close typological dating that could be applied to the artefactual material recovered.

Consequently, although the start- and end-dates of occupation are reasonably clear, and mainly defined by artefactual evidence, the sub-phasing is somewhat interpretative, and driven as much by plausible spatial relationships as demonstrable stratigraphy supported by artefactual dating.

Gravel Storage Area

The topsoil was removed by machine under archaeological supervision. To the north and south of the gravel ridge, a subsoil layer was exposed. Features were identified cutting the gravel or the subsoil, and were provisionally accorded a Saxon or medieval date, on the basis of surface finds or their spatial proximity/alignment to known features within the excavation areas to the west (Lot's Hole) and south (Lake End Road West). None of the identified archaeological features was excavated, in line with the brief's recommendation that the archaeology be preserved *in situ* if possible.

Eleven test pits were excavated through this subsoil layer to assess its depth and to determine the potential for any sealed archaeological horizons. Details of the results from the test pits are to be found on the CD-ROM. The archaeological results are incorporated into the corresponding descriptive and interpretative sections of the adjacent excavations.

The investigative procedure adopted on this area provided a retrospective check on the reliability of the methodology adopted on the earlier excavations, which is considered to be particularly critical in the interpretation of the middle Saxon deposits.

Recording

The recording procedure adopted on all of the OAU excavations followed standard practice (Wilkinson 1992). However, context, small find and sample numbers were often duplicated on adjacent sites, so a post-excavation prefix was assigned to each site. Details of all the site codes and context numbers can be found on the CD-ROM. As far as the three major sites covered by this volume are concerned, the prefixes are as follows:

Lake End Road East   Prefix 30,000
Lake End Road West   Prefix 40,000
Lot's Hole   Prefix 50,000

Thus context 415 becomes 50415 at Lot's Hole (DLH 96), 40415 at Lake End Road West (LERW 97) and 30415 at Lake End Road East (DOLER 96). The prefixes also apply to the small find and soil sample numbers.

Chapter 2:   Archaeological and Historical Background

by Jonathan Hiller and Julian Munby

ARCHAEOLOGICAL BACKGROUND
by Jonathan Hiller

In 1998, it was suggested that the results of the two projects be published together as a series of monographs. The linking of the two projects involved the identification of a loosely defined study area that extended from just below Cookham, immediately upriver from Maidenhead, to Windsor, and encompasses a 2–3 km wide corridor of the river plain (see Fig. 2.1). The sites within the area targeted for archaeological fieldwork and considered in this volume were bounded to the north by the M4 and to the south by the River Thames.

Topography, geology and environment

The topography is generally level and represents part of the Thames Valley floodplain (Fig. 2.1). Locally the site at Lot's Hole (NGR SU 9220 7970) lies at 23 m OD and is situated immediately south of the M4. To the south-east the two sites of Lake End Road East and Lake End Road West (NGR SU 929 796) lie at 22 m OD, and are separated by the B2306 (known locally as Lake End Road) (see Fig. 2.1). The area is generally level terrain, and modern land use has been principally as open fields devoted to market gardening and cereal agriculture. The site of the Eton College Rowing Course is generally level terrain, and comprised open fields adjacent to the River Thames.

The geology of the study area comprises first terrace river gravels of the Pleistocene (Sherlock 1947, 54). The gravel consists 'mainly of flint with subsidiary quartzite sandstone and chert' (Jarvis *et al.* 1984, 14). Overlying the gravel are areas of alluvial silt, formed during periods of flood activity. Relict watercourses cross the study area, and have done so until comparatively recently: two water channels or ditches are depicted on John Rocque's map of Berkshire published in 1761 (Pl. 2.1), and these survive today as managed drainage channels. The map shows the channels cutting across the meadows and fields surrounding Lake End Green and the village of Dorney, before converging as one, to join the River Thames to the east of Boveney.

The flood alleviation channel extends through part of an area that in the prehistoric period was interlaced by ancient stream and river courses crossing the low-lying ground creating gravel islands or eyots along the line of the Thames Valley. These islands were fertile and were favoured locations for prehistoric activity and settlement (see: Eton Rowing Lake, Allen and Welsh 1996; Southwark, Yule 1988; for a general discussion see Lambrick 1992). Through time, as the alignment of the River Thames became more stabilised, settlements like Dorney, with Boveney and Eton Wick to the south-east have all been established on the higher gravel islands, bounded to the north and south by large areas of alluvium.

The soil types in the area of Bray, Dorney and Eton Wick, all close to the present line of the Thames tend to be shallow and imperfectly drained sandy clay loam, reflecting the influence of the floodplain evolution. The depth of topsoil/ploughsoil over the gravel is typically between 0.3 and 0.4 m; seasonal flooding is not infrequent. These areas are not suited for horticultural crops, though cereals and grasses are grown; the land is exploited as pasture. Upstream, at Boveney Lock and between Maidenhead and Dorney the soil types become sandier and the soils tend to be deeper (up to 0.76 m over gravel). Such land is suitable for arable crops and intensive market gardening, although it is also exploited as pasture.

The state of current knowledge

The following is a summary of the known archaeological background of the investigation area and the wider Thames Valley landscape, from the prehistoric to the post-medieval. Figure 2.2 shows all the locations of Anglo-Saxon findspots within the study area, as listed in the gazetteer (see Table 2.1).

The middle Thames has, until relatively recently, been the subject of comparatively little archaeological research. In 1975 a cropmark survey of the river gravels of the middle Thames Valley was published (Gates 1975). The survey was based on a review of aerial photographs, though little excavation or fieldwalking evidence was available to supplement the study. Since the mid 1970s further aerial photographs have become available, but in general the photographic coverage of the region has been poor, owing to local flying restrictions imposed by the proximity of Heathrow Airport. In the 1990s cropmarks within the general study area were plotted by the Aerial Reconnaissance section of the RCHME (now English Heritage) as part of their Survey of the Thames River Gravels. Figure 2.1 includes a compilation and interpretation of the current cropmark evidence. Several archaeological sites recognised by aerial photography had already been destroyed by the late 1970s by urban expansion and the construction of the M4 Motorway. Gravel extraction sites had also affected the archaeology of the region, a situation only partly mitigated by rescue excavations. Finds collected during gravel extraction south of the river Thames in the Bray area suggested the presence of Mesolithic, Neolithic, Iron Age and Roman archaeological activity in the vicinity.

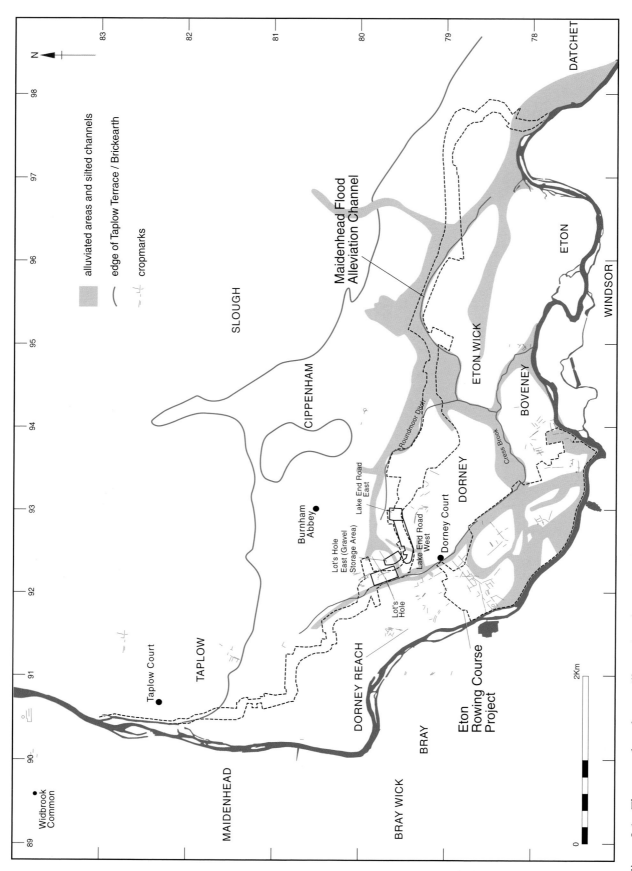

Figure 2.1 The general study area illustrating the topography, cropmarks, gravel islands and silted palaeochannels

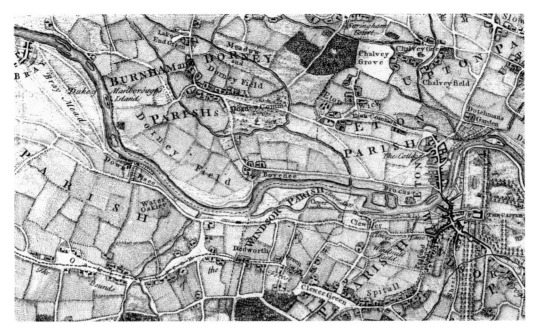

Plate 2.1 *Part of John Rocque's 1761 map of Berkshire, showing Dorney and Lake End Green*

In 1985, Buckinghamshire County Museum was commissioned by Thames Water to review the archaeological resources of the area between Maidenhead and Windsor and investigate the potential impact of any flood relief work. Photographs taken by the RCHME were reassessed, and a limited programme of archaeological fieldwalking was implemented. Attention was paid in particular to the area south and west of Dorney, which on the basis of the aerial photographic evidence was felt to be particularly vulnerable. The results (Carstairs 1986a) revealed that the study area was covered with a broad range of landscape features, gravel islands, relict watercourses and cropmarks. Finds from the fieldwalking suggested that archaeology of all periods could be expected on this part of the river plain (Carstairs 1986b).

Pre-Saxon activity

The prehistoric evidence for the area is considered in the companion volumes *Opening the wood, making the land*, and *Bridging the river, dividing the land*. Here reference is made only to Roman activity and to prehistoric monuments likely to have still been extant in the Saxon landscape.

A number of prehistoric burial monuments existed within the vicinity of the investigation areas (Fig. 2.1). These include a probable Neolithic mortuary enclosure just north of Dorney Reach, a possible causewayed enclosure just to the south and a second causewayed enclosure and mortuary enclosure, 3 km downriver, to the south of Eton Wick (Ford 1986; 1987). It is not certain just how visible these monuments were in the post-Roman landscape.

The pattern of Bronze Age burial in the middle Thames Valley appears to have been one of either isolated barrows or of small barrow groups, but spaced at frequent intervals (often no more than 1 km apart) across the landscape. A cropmark just north of Dorney Reach, thought to be a ring ditch, was destroyed during the construction of the M4, while two others have been excavated at Marsh Lane in advance of the construction of the Flood Alleviation Channel (see *Opening the wood, making the land*). The ring ditches of a further six barrows lie within the Eton College Rowing Course Project: these comprise a triple ring ditch adjacent to Queen's Eyot, a single ring ditch in the centre of the site, and a further group of four immediately south-west of Boveney (Fig. 1.4).

Other cropmark ring ditches are known to the north-west of Eton Wick and between Eton Wick and Eton itself (see cropmark survey plot in *Opening the wood, making the land*, and *Bridging the river, dividing the land*). A possible ring ditch was noted during small-scale excavations on Taplow Hill (G Fairclough pers. comm.). Most of these barrows could still have had upstanding mounds in the Saxon period. The most significant surviving prehistoric earthwork, however, was probably the rampart and ditch of Taplow Hillfort. Recent excavations here have demonstrated that the ditch was still some 1.5 m deep as late as the 7th century AD (Allen and Lamdin-Whymark 2000). The hilltop has also produced substantial evidence of settlement in the early and late Iron Age, continuing into the Roman period (Berkshire SMR 1542, 1546, and 1561).

Recent excavations, including those reported in *Bridging the river, dividing the land*, have considerably increased our understanding of Roman activity in the area. Middle to late Iron Age enclosed settlements

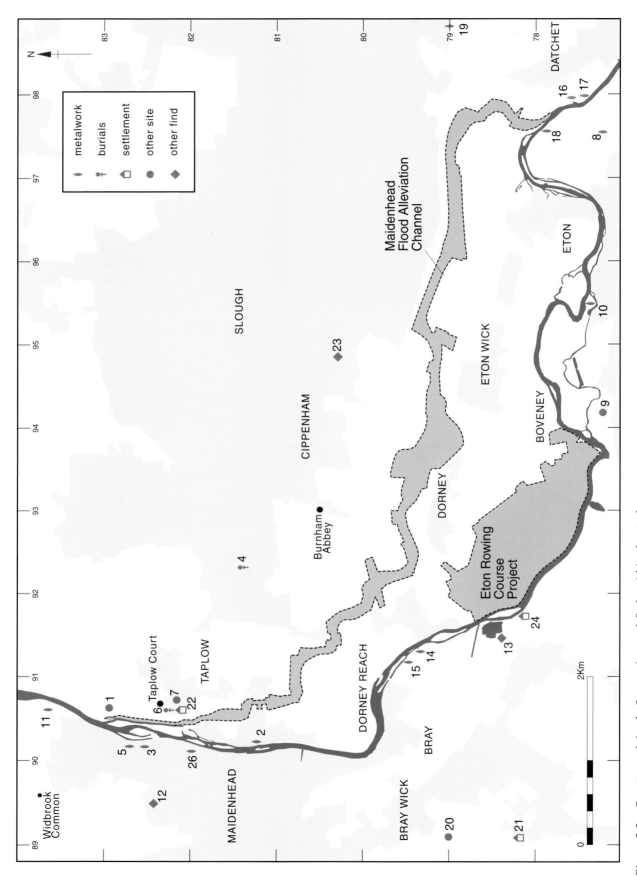

Figure 2.2 Gazetteer of Anglo-Saxon sites and finds within the study area

Table 2.1 *Gazetteer of Anglo-Saxon finds and sites in the study area*

Gaz No	Site Name	NGR	NMR Unique Identifier	SMR Number	Type	Description	References
1	Taplow	SU 906 829		Bucks 2929	Site, Find	Bapsey Pond, by tradition created by Saint Birinius, first bishop of Dorchester. An iron knife and skull have been found in the pond.	
2	Taplow	SU 901 813		Bucks 2294	Find	Late Anglo-Saxon spearhead, found in 1880s	
3	River Thames, above Boulter's Lock	SU 903 826		Bucks 1563	Find	Possible Late Anglo-Saxon axe head with some shaft still intact and covered with a bronze ferrule	
4	Hitcham	SU 9217 8119	251717 SU 98 SW 11		Site	An Anglo-Saxon inhumation, with shield and sword, was discovered in Windmill Field, Hitcham *c* 1890 during excavations for the GWR.	Maidenhead & Taplow FC 8th Annual Report (1890–91), 46
5	Ray Mill	SU 903 827		Berks 00308.00.000 – RW8013 Bucks 1441	Find	An axe of possible Anglo-Saxon date	Reading Museum Index Card
6	Taplow Barrow	SU 9061 8216	251689 Event 641694 SU 98 SW 3	Bucks 1542 SAM 18	Site	Taplow Barrow is a 7th century Anglo-Saxon round-barrow burial. Grave goods included three shields, three spearheads, two buckets, a Coptic bronze bowl, glass vessels, drinking horns, a sword, a gold buckle, gold belt clasps and bone draught pieces	VCH Bucks 1 (1905), 199
7	Taplow	SU 907 821			Site	Taplow Saxon church Parch marks have revealed the site of a small Anglo-Saxon church with apse and side *porticus*. Its shape is sugges-tive of a pre-Viking origin	Stocker and Went 1995
8	The Crown, Windsor Rd., Slough, Berks.	SU 975 797		Berks 00206.00.000 – SL 7864	Find	Late Anglo-Saxon spearhead	Wymer 1959, 124
9	Windsor Marina	SU 932 772		Berks 04177.00.000 – RW14942	Find	A dump of material probably dredged from the Thames from caravan park near Windsor Marina. It includes human remains, a leather shoe and animal bone. A late Anglo-Saxon date has been suggested, but the date is uncertain	
10	Clewer	SU 955 774		Berks 00196.01.000 – RW7837	Find	Anglo-Saxon spear recovered from the Thames.	
11	River Thames, near Maidenhead Court	SU 907 837		Berks 00319.00.000 – RW8024	Find	Early Anglo-Saxon spearhead	Rutland and Greenaway 1971–2
12	58 Summer-leaze Rd., Maidenhead	SU 895 824	248555 SU 88 SE 49	Berks 00611.00.000 – RW8380	Find	An Anglo-Saxon bead.	Rutland and Greenaway 1969
13	Bray	SU 915 784		Berks 00128.00.000 – RW7662	Find	Sherds of Late Anglo-Saxon/Norman coarse grey sandy ware found in gravel pit	

Table 2.1 *(Continued)*

Gaz No	Site Name	NGR	NMR Unique Identifier	SMR Number	Type	Description	References
14	River Thames, at Bray	SU 9131 7945	251269 SU 97 NW 11		Find	An Anglo-Saxon sword, dragged from the Thames between Bray Mill and Monkey Island in 1855.	Peake 1931, 183
15	River Thames, at Bray	SU 916 785	251311 SU 97 NW 27		Find	A Late Saxon spearhead (also described as Viking) found in the Thames below the Cut at Bray in March 1951. On loan to Reading Museum (Acc. No. 65:51)	
16	River Thames, at Windsor	SU 9790 7748	251072 SU 97 NE 27		Find	An Anglo-Saxon iron spearhead was recovered from the River Thames under Victoria Bridge, Windsor	Peake 1931, 245
17	River Thames, at Windsor	SU 9793 7736	251091 SU 97 NE 34		Find	An Anglo-Saxon iron spearhead was dredged from the Thames below Victoria Bridge in June 1935	
18	Windsor Road, Slough	SU 9758 7983	251173 SU 97 NE 64		Find	Anglo-Saxon/Viking spearhead found during alterations to The Old Crown Hotel, Slough,	
19	Datchet	SU 99 79	251217 SU 97 NE 108		Find	An Anglo-Saxon *sceatta* was found in a garden east of the village of Datchet. Series × (Type 31) dated to 675–750.	Hill and Metcalf 1984
20	Moor Farm, Holyport	SU 891 790		Berks 00464.01.000 – RW772	Structure	Excavations revealed a series of pointed stakes at 1.5m intervals driven into a peat deposit. The timbers were dated to 753 +/− 155 AD by radio-carbon dating	
21	Moor Farm, Holyport	SU 891 782	247991 Event 628129 Event 628126 SU 87 NE 30 SU 87 NE 17		Site	Anglo-Saxon and medieval settlement site and barn.	Maidenhead Arch & Hist Soc Newsletter May-June (1983), 6–7
22	Taplow Court	SU 906 822	Event 1116056 1116113 SU 98 SW 5		Site	Surveys in 1996 showed that St Nicholas Church, Taplow Court had its origins in the Anglo-Saxon period.	
23	Brook Farm	SU 948 803	Event 1250542		Find	Anglo-Saxon pottery was found during excavations at Brook Farm in 1995.	
24	Hoveringham Pit	SU 918 781	Event 627956 SU 97 NW 43		Site	Anglo-Saxon settlement and metal production furnace.	Rutland and Greenaway 1970
25	River Thames, near Maidenhead	SU 90 82	251765 251775 251792 SU 98 SW 25 SU 98 SW 29 SU (* SW 36		Find	Anglo-Saxon spears.	Peake, 1931, 126, 211

known at Cippenham and the Eton College Rowing Course both continued to flourish through the early Roman period (Ford 1998; Allen and Welsh 1996). A group of Iron Age and Roman enclosures with evidence of farmstead activity was found during the Flood Alleviation Scheme excavations north-west of Dorney and another such linear group of enclosures was discovered by geophysical survey, trenching and excavation at Agars Plough, near Eton (Ford 1991; OAU 1998; see also *Bridging the river, dividing the land* of this series, and Chapter 2, this volume). Another enclosure visible as a cropmark just north of Dorney Common was interpreted as Roman, but fieldwalking has not confirmed this interpretation (Carstairs 1986b, 167). Nevertheless, it can be seen that there is a relatively high density of Iron Age/ Roman rural farmsteads on the gravel terraces in this part of the Thames Valley. There are no Roman large towns in the immediate investigation area, but the substantial small town of Staines was situated 10 km to the east of the investigation areas (Fig. 1.1).

All of the early Roman rural sites mentioned above were abandoned by the end of the 3rd century AD, and there is less evidence of late 4th-century Roman settlement in the area. A late Roman cemetery was partly excavated immediately south of the Thames at Bray by the Middle Thames Archaeological Society, during gravel extraction in the 1960s. At least 21 burials including 7 cremations were recovered. A large quantity of occupation material of 3rd and 4th-century date was also found, suggesting that there was a settlement nearby (Anon. 1970; Anon. 1971; Wilson 1972; Stanley 1972). The villa at Cox Green, Maidenhead appeared to be occupied and periodically developed from the 2nd century through to the 4th century (Bennett 1962). Romano-British pottery and other finds were found during groundworks at Taplow Cricket Ground between 1954 and 1956, but there is no record of any associated features (SMR 1561).

Saxon activity

In the Upper and Lower Thames Valley, the majority of Anglo-Saxon settlements are confined to the higher gravel terraces. Saxon settlement evidence remains scarce along the river plain between Cookham and Windsor (Fig. 2.2 & Table 2.1). It is known that the Roman cemetery at Bray was overlain by occupation levels of early Saxon date, while the Thames Conservancy Records provide interesting details about the nature of Saxon activity along this particular stretch of the Thames (see Table 2.1). A spearhead of 6th century date was recovered from the river at Cliveden in 1932 (Bucks Acc. No. 280: 41).

Mortuary sites also provide evidence for middle Saxon activity. A large round barrow excavated at Taplow near Maidenhead in 1882 contained a burial evidently of some status, is as it was accompanied with shields, glass vessels and a gold buckle; the burial is dated to the 7th century (Fig. 2.2 no. 6). Other probable Saxon burials have been found on the hilltop,

most recently an extended inhumation accompanied by a knife (Allen and Lamdin-Whymark 2000, 25–6). A Saxon burial with shield and sword was found in a field near Hitcham (Fig. 2.2 no. 4) only 2 km north of Lake End Road. Other Saxon burials are known at the monastic site at Cookham, Berkshire, which was founded in the early 8th century (SMR 505, Peake 1931). An inhumation cemetery was discovered at Bourne End, Wooburn (Bucks) in the 1850s, during the construction of a railway there. The finds included swords, knives and spearheads, which were dated to the 7th and 8th centuries.

A knife blade (scramasax) of 8th-century date was found at Magna Carta Island, Runnymede in 1934 (Berks Acc. No. 283: 47), and late Saxon spearheads are known from below Cut, Bray (1951, Berks Acc. No. 65: 51); from between Maidenhead Bridge and Boulter's Lock (Fig. 2.2 no. 28; 1954, Berks Acc. No. 33: 54) and from near Staines (Berks Acc. No. 61: 54, 1954). A winged spearhead of 9th to 11th-century date was found at Cookham in 1958 (Berks Acc. No. 327: 58).

A source of evidence for middle and later Saxon activity comes from ecclesiastical sites such as the minsters that were established along the Thames Valley. Of these, it appears that with the notable exception of the Minster at Cookham near Maidenhead, most were located at opposite ends of the Thames Valley (Blair 1996, 16). The site at Cookham (*Cocheham*) near Maidenhead was certainly developed by the 8th century, and may be associated with the defended *burh* of *Sceattesege* (Ford 1987, 99). Other sites include a possible early church at Taplow, while it is claimed that St Nicholas Church, Taplow is of Saxon origin (Fig. 2.2 nos 7 & 22).

Further afield, a small village or farmstead is postulated south-west of the church at Old Windsor, which is thought to have been active in the first half of the 8th century on the basis of the pottery evidence and the features discovered there; by the 9th century there had been major changes at the site, and it was apparently of some status with stone buildings. These buildings were interpreted as part of a water mill, with 3 vertical wheels served by a substantial leat some 6 m wide and up to 3 m deep. The finds suggest that at least one of the buildings may have had a tiled roof and glazed windows. The published evidence so far indicates that the mill suffered a fire in the late 9th or 10th century (OAU 1996, 3). By the early 11th century the palace of Old Windsor was a royal residence of Edward the Confessor (Wilson and Hurst 1958).

Other sites lying beyond the limit of the study area include traces of later Saxon settlements and activity at Shepperton Green (Canham 1979), Stanwell (Poulton 1978) and Staines (Drewett, Rudling and Gardiner 1988, 294). The status of these settlement sites and the nature of the occupation evidence remain unclear, however, as the excavation areas have been generally on a small scale. Nonetheless, it appears that in the middle to late Saxon period, the middle Thames region was characterised by a number of small farmstead-type settlements along the line of the River Thames, making use of the fertile tributaries that extended both north and south of the river. No evidence for a major inland fair town, or *wic*, has yet been discovered, though the extent and size of the potential settlements at Old Windsor and Taplow are still not fully understood. Recently a double spiral-headed pin, pottery and a probable building were found at Taplow Court, suggesting late 7th-century occupation close to the burial mound (Allen and Lamdin-Whymark 2000, 25–6; 2001, 286–9).

HISTORICAL BACKGROUND: DOCUMENTARY AND PLACE-NAME EVIDENCE
by Julian Munby

The landscape of Eton and Dorney forms a very distinct element of south Buckinghamshire, where a series of gravel 'islands' in the Thames river plain have become discrete settlements, and where the courses of former river channels will have influenced every phase of transformation, and still influence the present landscape (Fig. 2.1). While this area can be studied on its own, and has now been subject to a very searching campaign of archaeological interventions, it must also be placed in a wider context. Leaving aside the possible connections with the Berkshire south side of the Thames, the Eton/Dorney area can be seen as the tail end of the 'Burnham Plateau' region, a distinct area at the back of the Chilterns with a linear arrangement of historic settlements reaching from the higher gravel terrace to the north down to the river Thames at the south end of the region. The links between the very extensive areas of riverside meadow and the almost limitless areas of woodland pasture in the hills must have been a factor in human settlement and land use in this locality long before it was attested in Domesday Book.

A general survey of the potential for the landscape history of the Dorney/Eton area was undertaken by Dr Jonathan Hunn in 1997, which comprised a search of map and other documentary sources, resulting in a plotting of basic historic landscape elements, and identification of several themes for investigation (1997). Since then, a further search has been undertaken on potential sources in the archives at Dorney Court and Eton College. The key visual sources for the landscape history are the early estate maps of Dorney (1812 – Buckinghamshire Record Office, Ma/63/4T) and Eton (1742 – Eton Archives S1/135), which show local land use and ownership in Dorney, Boveney and Eton. In the wider area the post-medieval extent of commons and greens is clearly depicted on the Ordnance Survey drawing (OSD 153) of 1811, and the one-inch map (Sheet 7) published in 1822. The historic parish boundaries are depicted on first edition 6-inch OS maps (1875–83) along with much topographical detail. The manorial histories given in the *Victoria County History* reveal

links between detached areas, which only gradually acquired separate manorial or parish status.

The regional context *(Fig. 2.3)*

The grouping of historic parishes in geographical zones is of known relevance for the historic period, when manors and parishes were often coterminous, and the full extent of the parish was exploited. The area shown in Figure 2.3 includes all the historic parishes coterminous with Dorney and Eton on the north side of the Thames.

These estates, which apart from Burnham and Boveney were single estates in each parish, all had modest amounts of meadow, very significant amounts of woodland, and thriving fisheries (Campbell 1971). They demonstrated a consistent pattern of land use as a series of long parishes extending from the flood plain up to the Chilterns, with woods and commons at the north end, and villages sited at approximately the 45 m contour. The northern ends of the parishes are all on glacial sands and gravels, with the villages on or near the edge of the gravel (Boyn Hill) terrace. The southern ends of the parishes (together with the parish of Upton-cum-Chalvey) span the lower gravel (Taplow) terrace and the lowest (Flood Plain) terrace. The settlement pattern of this area is less distinct, with numerous hamlets, often with village greens (Burnham Abbey and Cippenham in Burnham; Chalvey Green, Slough and Upton in Chalvey/Upton; Stoke Green in Stoke and Wexham).

The wide river plain has accommodated two riverside parishes, Dorney and Eton, together with the 'Liberty' of Boveney. It is especially notable that Dorney, Boveney and Eton continue the scattered settlement pattern: the last with Eton Wick at the west end of the parish, and Dorney/Boveney with a straggling settlement round its extensive and irregular village green. The riverside settlements also had links to the north: the 'Liberty' of Boveney was a chapelry of Burnham, and Dorney retained a long detached portion in Burnham (with its Dorney Wood adjacent to Boveney Wood up at the north end); the manor of Eton comprised areas that later became the separate parishes of Wexham and Hedgerley, with extensive commons and woodlands.

The shape of the hundreds also reflects the linearity of settlements, in as much as this end of the county is divided between Stoke Hundred in the south-east corner, and then the broad strip of land that forms Burnham Hundred, extending up to Chesham and Amersham on the Hertfordshire border. Outside of the area mapped on Figure 2.3 there are further links from low-lying estates to outlying portions of these hundreds in the Chilterns, most of which do not appear separately in Domesday Book and must therefore have been included under the main manor. Thus in Burnham Hundred, Taplow (anomalous as a long and riverside parish), had an outlier in Penn, Burnham originally included the parish of Beaconsfield, and Farnham had an

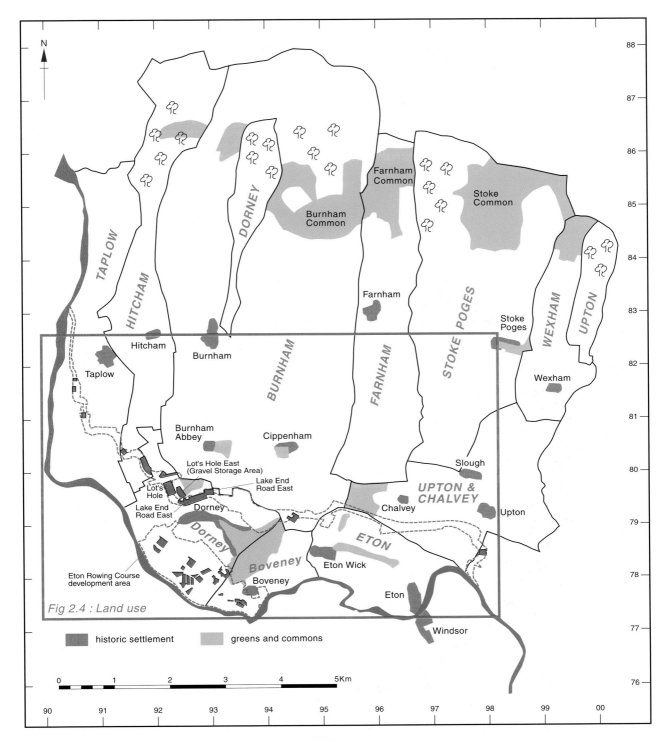

Figure 2.3 *Parishes and land use in the Dorney — Chilterns area*

outlier at Seer Green (Chenevix Trench 1973). In Stoke Hundred, as already mentioned, the manor of Eton included Wexham and Hedgerley; Upton had a further outlying portion between Hedgerley and Fulmer; the riverside parishes of Datchet and Wraysbury included the whole of Fulmer and Langley Marish respectively, while Iver had an outlying portion at Iver Heath.

This may suggest that in origin the riverside estates were part of long Chiltern-foot estates, which then became fossilised as late Saxon parishes. There is almost nothing in the early tenurial history to indicate the existence of large estates that were subsequently divided, and the distribution of pre-Conquest owners recorded in Domesday Book forms no more of a regular pattern than the diversity of holders in 1086. So it may be that the apparent confusion of divided estates/parishes with outlying portions does in fact reflect the ancient arrangements with discrete estates having distant grazing rights in the Chilterns. This of course would have been little different from the traditional arrangement of grazing access all round the Weald in Kent and Sussex, and the means of dividing wood or marsh pasture between adjacent settlements in other parts of England. But it does mean that the long-distance links between the Thames-side and Chilterns cannot be ignored for the medieval period, and may well have been relevant in earlier times.

The local context

Dorney, Boveney and Eton were all influenced by their geographical and geological setting, as a series of low gravel islands, surrounded by alluvium. The former river channels that (elsewhere in the Thames Valley) often disappear altogether, have here survived as hay meadows or pasture; and in contra-distinction to what is often found in medieval villages, the commons occur in the centre of the village and the arable fields are marginal, even occurring alongside the River Thames. The whole area is flat, with a recent (Pleistocene) geology of flood-plain gravel and alluvium, overlain with more or less well-drained soils that now have a range of classifications.

The early medieval landscape

Despite the absence of detailed evidence concerning the Saxon landscape, certain elements appear to pre-date the Norman Conquest. There are no Anglo-Saxon charters for this area, apart from one for Datchet (Sawyer 1968, no. 1454), and the Domesday evidence, summarised above, is of limited use on its own. However the boundaries of ancient parochial units as shown on mid to late 19th-century maps can be combined with what is known of later manorial and administrative history, so as to distinguish the probable limits of the earliest estates (Young 1979).

The significance of the cartographic evidence is that it records boundary information that is generally of known duration and stability. That is, the ecclesiastical parishes are of some considerable antiquity, dating from at least the 10th/11th centuries and in some cases even earlier. There is now widespread acceptance that the boundaries of ancient parishes were themselves based on pre-existing estate or communal units, which might represent the whole 'manor' or single estate, or a 'vill' or township consisting of more than one estate. In this instance, the number of Domesday manors is clear enough, and the main question is the territorial extent of their holdings.

Secondly, it is worth observing the character of the boundaries themselves. In contrast to the other 'estates', Eton is the only area that can make a claim to what can be described as a 'natural territory'. That is, it was defined by the River Thames on its southern and eastern sides, by the combined water courses of the Boveney and Roundmoor Ditches on its western side and by the Chalvey Ditch and Willow Brook on its northern side. Dorney's northern boundary continues like Eton's, skirting the meadows along the Roundmoor Ditch, but a detached portion of the Liberty of Boveney and parts of Burnham lay on the southern edge of the water course. On the north-west the boundary between the southern extremity of Hitcham and the north-western extremity of Dorney exhibits the classic characteristics of artificial imposition, stepping across the furlongs of fields or meadows. On the eastern side, the boundary between Dorney and Lower Boveney was comparatively straight and regular, but may be an arbitrary line: two thirds of its course crosses Dorney Green while the southern-most third was independent of any upstanding features (excluding trees) and it would seem most probable that this area had been common pasture since far back in antiquity. The south and western boundary of Dorney follows the course of the River Thames with one slight exception. At the north-west corner there was a small portion of the Berkshire parish of Bray that lay on the eastern side of the river. To what extent this represents a shift in the course of the river is difficult to say. One needs to remember that before the middle of the 19th century the Thames (except when it was in flood) rarely provided much of a barrier to movement due to its comparative shallowness.

The Boveney area is an anomaly, being a 'Liberty' (or exempt jurisdiction) within the parish of Burnham, one of the long Chiltern-edge parishes already discussed. According to the *Victoria County History* the parish would appear to have consisted of nine such Liberties (Boveney, Britwell, Brittilthrupp, Burnham, East Burnham, Cippenham, Lent, Weston and Woodland (later Wood). There is only one 'Liberty' which may be ascribed a definite area: Boveney was described as having an area of 463.6 acres (187.61 ha) with three detached portions. The largest of these was at Lake End north of Dorney, where the area was some 19.6 acres (7.94 ha); there was a small parcel adjacent on the north side of Roundmoor Ditch (approx. 5 acres) and one other a short distance to the north about 15.6 acres (6.34 ha) on the 1842 tithe map. These last two parcels were not included in the area of Boveney in *c* 1881. What is also curious is that although Boveney was part of the parish of Burnham, it does not appear to have been included on the Tithe map of 1842. However, the Burnham 'Liberties' appear to have been 'tithings' in the 14th century according to the court rolls (British Library, MS, Egerton 8326-8327; Bucks RO D 11/3/4). That is to say the subdivisions of the vill that formed the smallest unit of communal policing known as 'frankpledge'. What is more certain is that Boveney was a separate manor, appearing on its own in Domesday Book and with a continuous recorded descent (*VCH* 1925). The lack of parochial status for Boveney may well originate in its other Domesday estate, the single hide held by Reinbald the Priest as part of the church of Cookham (in Berkshire). Otherwise the historic churches, possibly of pre-Conquest origin, were to be found at Taplow, Dorney and Eton. That of Dorney was adjacent to the manor house, and the other two within their main respective settlements.

Domesday Book records the names of the late Anglo-Saxon landholders together with a summary of the value and components of their holdings. Although it is not possible to reconstruct the physical layout of the landscape it is possible to make some comparisons between the different entries. Population figures are not very informative, being essentially the count of manorial tenants, but only one villager is listed for Boveney, with totals of 24 for Taplow, 11 each for Dorney and Hitcham, 37 for Burnham, 26 for Upton and 21 for Eton.

The statistics for arable land are contained in the statement 'land for so many ploughs'. It has been recently argued that these figures are not an abstract terminology but are, on the whole, a broadly accurate reflection of the arable resources of a particular locality (Higham 1990, 36). This being so then it is also possible to make comparisons between the different estates (Boveney is treated as a single holding). An examination of the figures reveals that Dorney had the lowest area of arable (as measured by the number of ploughs) at 3 ploughlands. By contrast Boveney had 3.5 and in ascending order came Hitcham (6), Eton (8), Upton (10), Burnham (15) and Taplow with 16 ploughlands. What is interesting is that a high number of ploughlands did not necessarily translate into a high valuation. For example, using the 1086 valuations, it would appear that Taplow at 16 ploughlands was valued at £8 in contrast to Hitcham's 6 ploughlands (£4) and Burnham's 15 ploughlands (£10). Of course, it would be over-simplistic to assume that different land areas had different value in terms of their soil quality and productivity. Nevertheless, it is possible to compare the bald statistics for the number of villagers given above with the overall value of their associated estate.

With regard to the meadow resources, both Dorney and Burnham each had meadow for 3 ploughs but their combined area was only equal to that of East Burnham (6). Interestingly, Boveney also had meadow for 3 ploughs, which were more than the combined resources of Taplow and Hitcham (at 1 each) and more than either Eton or Upton (2 each). Of particular interest is the unusual mention of horse pasture at Dorney, especially in the context of the later stud farm at Cippenham (see below). The outlying wood pastures have already been discussed. One of the surprises of the Domesday data is the apparent lack of water mills from the area. Only Eton (valued at 20s) and Upton (1 valued at 4s) have mills recorded. Why Taplow, given its proximity to the Thames, should have no mill recorded is particularly surprising.

The later medieval landscape *(Pls 2.1–2)*

The evidence for the landscape in the medieval period is derived from a variety of sources most of which are either of late medieval or post-medieval date. It is, therefore, necessary to be cautious in interpreting the data and avoid the temptation of projecting it further back in time than the evidence will support. Nevertheless, it is clear that many landscape elements are not prone to sudden alterations without some compelling reason to change and are of considerable antiquity. The principal problem remains one of identifying the origin of field systems that have gradually evolved over a considerable period of time.

Meadow land was one of the most valuable types of land use in the medieval period and its availability and distribution was fundamental to the pattern of landholding in the medieval village. This was governed by local topography, both in terms of its drainage pattern, its exposure to flooding, and the character and quality of the soils. Of particular importance in this part of the Thames valley is the aspect of drainage and flooding. It is apparent that those areas adjacent to watercourses (Lake End/Roundmoor Ditch, Cresswell/Boveney Ditch and the ditch from Amerden Grove to the south) were where the principal meadows were located. It is one of the peculiarities of the local landforms here that the meadows in Taplow, Dorney and Eton run through the open fields along existing or former watercourses. While grazing animals were rigorously excluded from hay meadows prior to harvest, the rough pasture was potentially open all the time, and was generally on lower grade land. As has been previously observed, the scattered nature of settlement has resulted in many small areas of pasture (West Town Common, Lake End Green) in addition to larger areas such as Dorney Green, which was adjacent to (and undivided from) Boveney Green.

The arrangement of arable land was probably already well established by the time of Domesday, and it is likely that it then consisted of predominantly large open fields subdivided into furlongs, with manorial tenants having scattered holdings of individual strips, and crops rotated between the fields. A key element of the system was the opening of the fields after harvest for grazing, and the availability not only of allotted shares of meadow, but also grazing in those meadows after the hay harvest. This system is likely to have evolved over time although certain elements (particularly the open fields) would have required a degree of planning in the allocation of strips to members of the community. Whether they originated as a combination of piecemeal colonisation and shareholding, or as a single act of creation by the lord of the manor, the end result is much the same, and any evidence of origins hard to detect.

Despite the unevenness of the quality of the documents it has been possible to recreate some of the principle elements of the medieval landscape

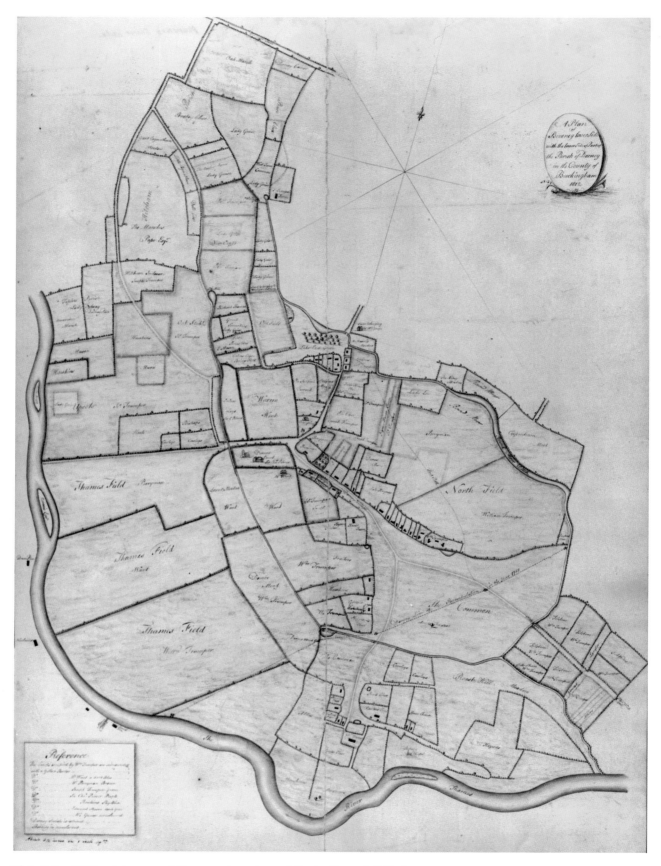

Plate 2.2   1812 estate map of Boveney (courtesy of Bucks Record Office)

(Figs 2.3–4). The information is derived from both medieval and post-medieval sources whose stability through their continued use is probable, rather than absolutely certain. The detail concerning the smaller land parcels is uncertain, but for the majority of the larger fields the information is broadly accurate.

The first observation to make is that all the larger field units would have been subdivided into long strip furlongs (some of which are recorded on later 18th and 19th-century maps). Secondly, that there were at least eight principal manorial holdings in the area (Taplow, Amerden, Huntercombe, Burnham Abbey, Dorney, Cippenham, Eton, Upton) and at least two other lesser manorial holdings (Weston, Boveney). These estates held land predominantly, but not exclusively, within their respective parochial areas. The extent to which some fields were inter-commoned by different manors has not been established. However, what is more probable is that individual holdings could become more dispersed among different manors. A relatively late arrival such as Burnham Abbey (founded in 1266) held the majority of its lands in the south of Burnham parish, but also had holdings in the manors of Eton and Dorney. The dower settlement of Lady Margaret de Huntercombe in AD 1368 listed lands held in Burnham, Dorney, Boveney and Eton (PRO C135/200/8). Dispersed holdings would have been regulated by the manorial court on whose lands they were situated. This is important to remember when considering the nature of medieval landscape as illustrated.

Although there were some eight 'manorial holdings' in the area under consideration, only two (Dorney and Eton) have their principal manorial extents shown (excluding the detached portion of Dorney). Therefore, it is only these two which may be described with any degree of completeness. Both Eton and Dorney possessed large open fields that were denoted by the terms 'north' and 'south'. The manor of Eton would appear to have been organised on a simple two-field system: that is, there would have been an equal distribution of strip holdings between fields and when one of them lay fallow (on alternate years) communal grazing would have been practised (Hall 1982, 19). The picture that emerges for Dorney is not so simple. Although the evidence is relatively late it would appear there were at least four principal arable fields. These were named as North Field, South Field, Thames Field and Upcote/Oak Stubbe (the last of these could be a late name so its medieval origin is not certain). In addition, there would appear to have been several closes to the north of Dorney church towards Lot's Mead and along the highway between Burnham and Dorney. At present we lack the information which would permit a detailed analysis of how the field system would have been regulated by the court leet of Dorney.

It would appear that the landscapes of Taplow and Upton were also arranged on a similar pattern of four or five large open fields operated under some

form of biannual rotation. However, this is conjecture and still remains to be demonstrated.

It is not certain how the lands of Boveney were arranged in the medieval period. It is possible that the names Roast or Rose Hill and Mulsharn or Moulsham indicate a two-field system, but this remains to be proved. The demesne lands of Burnham Abbey were scattered among at least six large common fields and were regulated through its own courts (PRO maps MR44–5).

The only other significant medieval landscape feature within the present study area was the enclosure known as 'Le Parke', a large irregular enclosure containing a large moated site. This was first mentioned in 1272 and covered an area of some 308 acres (124.5 ha). It formed part of the manor of Cippenham, but by the mid 15th century was no longer mentioned in documentary sources. Originally it was used for the rearing and hunting of deer, but by the mid 14th century it was used as a stud farm by Edward III; meadow grasses were especially important for horse rearing (PRO C132/42 (1); *VCH* 1925, 174–5; Gladitz 1997, 151).

The post-medieval period and Parliamentary Enclosure

The landscape of the early post-medieval period is unlikely to have altered in any dramatic way, though no doubt subtle changes did take place. Although there was a continual change in the pattern of land holding, this did not necessarily result in change to the landscape. An important influence on the maintenance of field systems depended, to a large extent, on the continuing authority of the manorial courts. This authority would have made it less easy to amalgamate an individual's holdings without the agreement of the court leet. Nevertheless, enclosure has been studied in the adjacent area of the Chiltern Hills (Roden 1969) where a phase of enclosure of common fields and common wastes between *c* 1550–1800 by agreement was followed by early 19th-century parliamentary enclosure that completed the process.

Eton and Dorney were slightly exceptional in this respect and, like Burnham, were never enclosed by act of parliament. Eton had only a small portion of its landscape un-enclosed by 1773. There was an agreement to enclose Pound Green at Dorney in 1790. By the time Dorney was first partially represented by cartographic means in 1808, and by the 1st edition one inch Ordnance Survey in 1811–22, there were no remains of any subdivided open fields. In the parish of Burnham and Upton, enclosure appears to have begun in the early 16th century according to the Inquisitions of depopulation (Eton: Bucks RO Ma R/19; Dorney: NRA 2613 serial no 260 and map Bucks RO Ma/63/2T; Burnham: Leadam 1897).

In the parish of Burnham the subdivided open fields survived for longer into the 19th century but here, as in Dorney and Eton, the enclosure movement had been proceeding on a piecemeal basis for some considerable time (probably over the course of

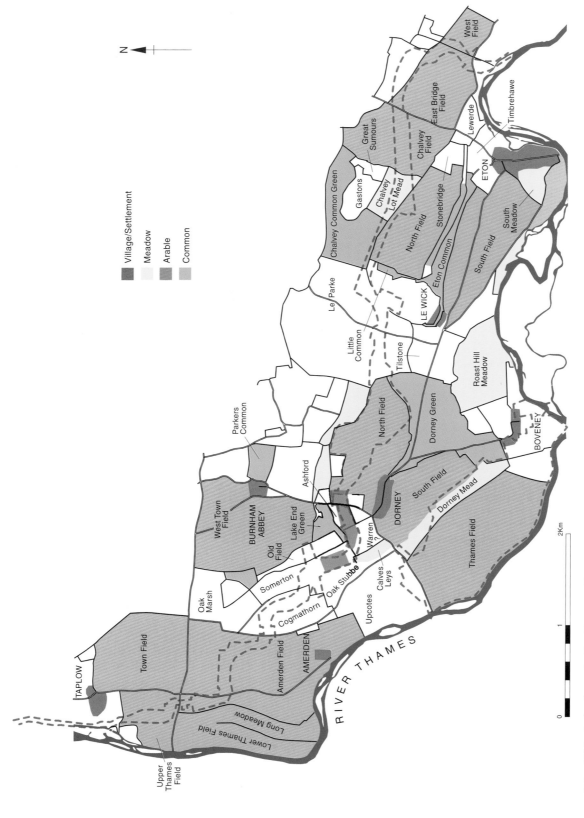

Figure 2.4 Historic land use in the Eton — Dorney area

Village/Settlement

Meadow

Arable

Common

several centuries). In the mid 17th century an area of common waste was enclosed in Taplow, and there were Parliamentary Enclosure Acts for Taplow in 1779; Hitcham in 1778; Farnham Royal in 1821; Stoke Poges in 1810, and Upton in 1808. The proposal to enclose Dorney Common in 1869 was unsuccessful, and it survived to be registered in the 1960 s (Taplow: BL MS, Add 26071; Dorney: NRA 2613 serial no 723; in general, Tate 1978; *VCH* 1925 and maps in Bucks RO).

The modern landscape

The cartographic link with the landscapes of the past and those of the present are provided by the Enclosure and Tithe Apportionment maps of the late 18th and mid 19th centuries. On these and their supporting documentation were recorded the details of field names, ownership/occupancy, area, tithable value and sometimes distinguishing topographical features (for example water courses, pits and old structures). Their usefulness is further enhanced by the first edition large scale (25 inch) Ordnance Survey maps of *c* 1875–80, which link through to all modern maps. They demonstrate that the landscape was still predominantly rural in composition: all the original medieval settlements still retain a rural aspect, with the exception of Upton whose population had quadrupled by 1861 (Reed 1979, 229).

In 1873 the largest landholders were the Grenfell estate of Taplow Manor, the Duke of Sutherland and Westminster, Sir Charles Palmer (1482 acres) and Eton College with its 1007 acres (HMSO 1875). The size of individual farms and the number of labourers employed were recorded on the census returns from the middle of the century. The 20th-century landscape can be followed through modern mapping, and two detailed sources: the valuations and maps from Lloyd George's 'Domesday' of land ownership of 1909–10 in the PRO (see Short 1989) and the records of the national farm surveys of England and Wales undertaken between 1940–43 (PRO MAF 73/3/52–56, and MAF 32.)

Dorney: the immediate landscape

In the absence of detailed manorial records from the late medieval-early modern period, the Dorney map of 1812 (Pl. 2.2) is a key source for the local topography. This is 'A Plan of Boveney lower side, with the lower side of Part of the Parish of Dorney', and it gives field names and ownership, though the only indication of land use is the names themselves. The picture of Dorney given in the 1812 map will not necessarily show the extent of medieval settlement, though it is likely to reflect its character.

Houses

The most obvious feature of the map is the scattered nature of housing, spreading from near the church and manor house along either side of Dorney Green, and also around Lake End Green. In Boveney there is a smaller concentration on one side of the common. The majority of the Dorney properties have a regular 'toft' surrounding the house, as if they were traditional peasant holdings rather than being encroachments on the edge of the common. This is less certain with the houses at Lake End Green, which have more of the appearance of being latecomers, and possibly encroaching on a larger space. As has been observed, this dispersed settlement type is actually a feature of the local landscape, to be found in most of the adjacent parishes. The corollary of this is that the observed historic pattern may only be the end of a continual process, and it is not unlikely that earlier settlement may have come and gone in other places.

Thus the archaeological evidence for medieval settlement at Lot's Hole could be seen as settlement spreading along the trackway to the north, and indeed the evidence of Anglo-Saxon activity south of what became Lake End Green could be the precursor of later settlement on the Green here. The field names south of Lake End Green: 'Pin Ashford' and 'Ashford' are topographical ('pin' is likely to be from (animal) pen), but the two 'Somerton' names (Great and Little Somertons) south of Lot's Hole may be the name of a lost settlement.

Fields

The general distribution of fields has already been described, with 'North Field' and 'Thames Field' (although divided) representing the two main open arable fields. A line of meadows 'Dorney Mead', 'Lower Meadow' and 'Calves Leys' are likely to be the hay meadows, which at one time would have been allotted in strips. In 1812 these fields were largely divided between the tenancies of Perryman, Want and Trumper. This leaves a large number of closes at the north end of Dorney, which do not obviously fit into this pattern (although the 1812 map does include several parcels in Hitcham parish). They may have formed another field – it was not unusual for a three-field to become a two-field system – or been a separate demesne farm (much of it was held by J Trumper in 1812). Another possibility is that there was a separate hamlet: at Lot's Hole are a number of small paddocks that could represent earlier farms (their 'Somertons' names have been mentioned above), with an 'Old Field' immediately to the east, while further north along the track is 'West Farm Common' (named after West Town Farm in Burnham) that may imply a former settlement nearby.

It is evident that the watercourses (still in 1812 shown as open ditches) have formed this pattern of land use, but it is notable that at that date the two ditches originated as ponds or springs at their northern extremities, and flowed south towards the Thames, so they were no longer streams linked to the river at both ends.

Chapter 3:   The Anglo-Saxon Archaeology

by Jonathan Hiller and Simon Mortimer

THE FLOOD ALLEVIATION SCHEME

The detailed evidence from all three excavation sites and the two supplementary watching briefs can be found in the appropriate section of the CD-ROM. The evidence is summarised below.

Summary of the stratigraphy *(Figs 3.1–4 & 5.1)*
by Jonathan Hiller and Simon Mortimer

The full extent of the archaeological evidence is shown in Figure 5.1, in relation to paleochannels and probable areas of seasonal waterlogging. Detail of the Anglo-Saxon features is shown on Figures 3.1–3.3, and the range of identified pit types is shown in Figure 3.4.

The middle Anglo-Saxon archaeology from the three adjacent sites of Lot's Hole, Lake End Road West and Lake End Road East consists almost exclusively of pits. None of the excavated ditches, gullies or other boundaries could be attributed to the Anglo-Saxon period, though it is possible that some of the Roman boundaries could have survived in use until the middle Saxon period, as at Lake End Road West the pits appear to partly respect some droveways associated with the Roman field system.

Most of the pits were excavated into the gravel; there was some variation in both diameter and depth, although they averaged approximately 3–3.5 m diameter by 1.2–1.6 m deep, with evenly sloping sides.

The fills from the pits tended to display broadly similar characteristics. The basal fills usually consisted of clean, interleaved layers of silt and gravel, probably derived from natural erosion of the pit sides. Some contained humic elements, characteristic of cess. The central fills often exhibited well-defined tip lines, and in some cases displayed alternating clean gravel layers with layers of charcoal and bone-rich debris. The final layers typically comprised dark homogeneous deposits with few tip lines, containing artefacts and animal bones. Typical sections are illustrated in Figure 3.4.

Lake End Road West *(Fig. 3.1 & Pl. 3.1)*

A total of 90 pits (Pls 3.2–5) were distributed unevenly along the length of the site, but there was little evidence for any significant patterning. They were found mainly in the eastern two-thirds of the site, apparently avoiding the eastern edge of the area possibly prone to seasonal waterlogging, with only one discrete cluster of three pits identified at the far western end of the site (see Fig. 5.1). Within the main area of pit use there were subsidiary clusters, with spaces of 10–15 m between them, forming open north-south oriented corridors. Within each cluster the pits tended to be several metres apart from each other, although there was occasional intercutting.

The finds assemblage indicated some spatial evidence for organisation of activities; perhaps the most obvious was a concentration of iron slag from two pits in the west of the main area of pits. The bases of 42 smithing hearths were found from pit 40878 and 22 from 40668.

Lot's Hole *(Fig. 3.2)*

Twenty pits of middle Saxon date were found in this area, and a number of pits were revealed in the watching brief on the gravel storage area immediately to the east of the south end of the site. From finds recovered from the tops of these pits, at least four can be confidently assigned to the middle Saxon period. Again, no contemporary structural evidence was found, although a trackway, associated with the Romano-British settlement partially revealed on the Lake End Road West site, which ran north-south to the east of the excavation may still have been in use in this period. Most of the pits were found in the south-eastern part of the site, and appear to respect the east edge of the palaeochannel that crossed the south-western part of the site, though this was probably silted up by the Anglo-Saxon period.

Lake End Road East *(Fig. 3.3 & Pl 3.6)*

A total of 13 pits of Saxon date were identified at Lake End Road East (Pl. 3.6), including a possible alignment of four in the south-east corner (30588, 30647, 30521, 30620), as well as another tentative alignment in the south-west. Again, as in Lake End Road West, no structural evidence was identified. Three unexcavated pits seen in the Watching Brief area immediately to the south of the site were probably contemporary because they resembled known Anglo-Saxon pits in the excavation area.

Gravel Storage Area *(Fig. 3.2)*

A small number of archaeological features were exposed immediately beneath the topsoil as were two discrete finds scatters on the surface of the subsoil. The identified features included ten large pits or natural features, four of which were considered likely to be of middle Saxon date, and a single rectangular post-built structure and linear ditch thought to form parts of the medieval settlement at Lot's Hole. A posthole, eight possible

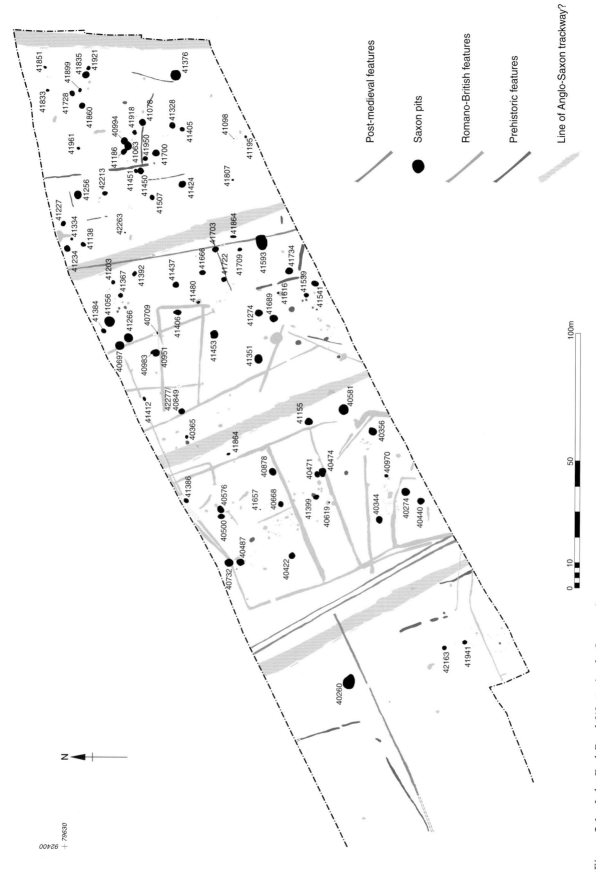

Figure 3.1 Lake End Road West: Anglo-Saxon pits

Figure 3.2 *Lot's Hole: Anglo-Saxon pits*

Figure 3.3 Lake End Road East: Anglo-Saxon pits

stakeholes and a large pit or hearth were found sealed by the subsoil in the northern part of the area. No archaeological features were found in the southern half of the area, though a possible palaeochannel was found sealed by the subsoil in the south-eastern corner.

Dating

The evidence for Anglo-Saxon activity fits broadly within a middle Saxon (7th-9th century) date range. Although occasional pot fragments show some similarities with earlier Anglo-Saxon parallels, overall the assemblage fits quite well in the slightly later period. Several ceramic types, notably Ipswich Ware and Tating Ware, belong firmly in the 8th or early 9th century. Other artefactual evidence, as well as radiocarbon dating, all confirms this date. There is occasional typological evidence for later activity, such as the 9th/10th-century bone comb (SF 42888 see Fig. 4.8 no. 2), but such activity appears to have been very sporadic.

THE ETON ROWING COURSE PROJECT

Apart from a single sherd of pottery recovered from Area 6, the only identified archaeological feature datable to the Saxon period was an isolated inhumation. In the interests of the coherence of the related information, the grave, skeleton, and finds are summarily described and discussed below.

Full descriptions of the grave and its contents can be found in the appropriate section of the CD-ROM.

The Anglo-Saxon grave from Boveney
(Figs 1.4 & 3.5)
by Angela Boyle, Peter Hacking, Tim Allen and Janet Ambers

A single grave 5842 containing skeleton 5844 was located towards the west end of Area 6. (see Fig. 1.4 for the location of the burial; the grave plan and grave goods are illustrated in Fig. 3.5) The grave, which survived to a depth of 0.12 m, had been truncated by ploughing and therefore most of the bones were damaged and some were missing. The body had been buried in a supine extended position with its head to the south.

The skeleton
by Peter Hacking

The skull was in small fragments with the exception of the right temporal and mandible. Cervical vertebrae 1, 2 and 4–6 were complete, but only fragments of the thoracic and lumber vertebrae survived. The ribs and sacrum were also fragmented and the upper arms were also very poorly preserved although both lower arms survived. The pelvis and legs were fragmented and the bones of the hands and feet were mostly absent. The skeleton was that of an adult, probably female; dental attrition suggested an age of approximately 35 years. The height of the individual was approximately 1.65 m.

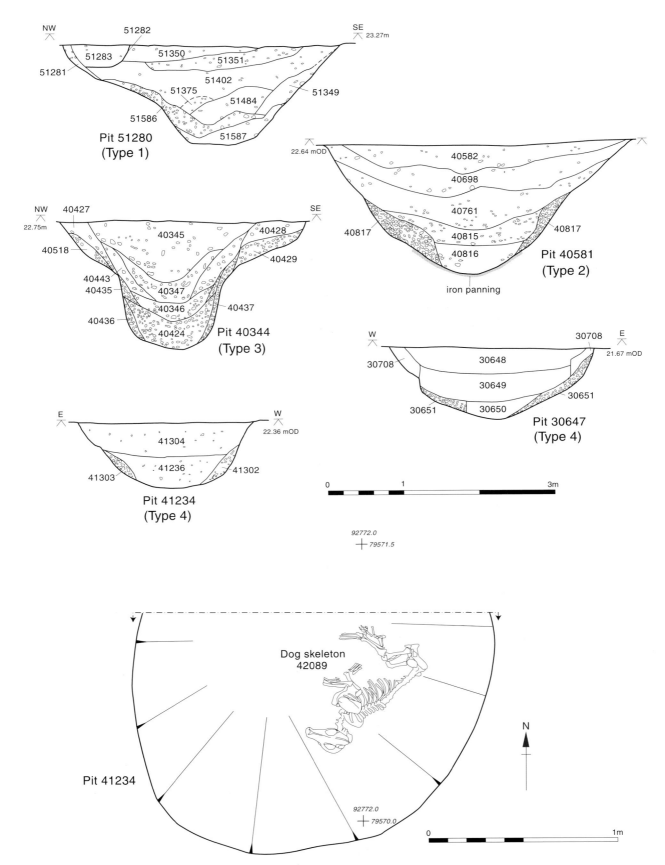

Figure 3.4   *Anglo-Saxon pits. The range of identified pit types and detail of the dog skeleton 42089*

Plate 3.1   Lake End Road West: during the excavation

The radiocarbon date
by Janet Ambers

A radiocarbon date of 1485 ± 40 BP (BM-3137; 430–660 cal AD at 2 sigma) was obtained on the right femur of the skeleton by the radiocarbon laboratory of the British Museum.

The grave goods
by Angela Boyle

A number of objects were located underneath the left pelvis. These included a copper alloy and amethyst pendant, a strip fragment, a plate and a disc, all copper alloy, along with two metal objects of uncertain func-

Plate 3.2   Lake End Road West: Anglo-Saxon pit 40274 under excavation

Plate 3.3   Lake End Road West: Anglo-Saxon pit 41234 under excavation

tion, one of lead and one of iron, and a bone rod. A broken silver ring fragment lay next to the mandible and had presumably been suspended around the neck. Struck flints and animal bone were also recovered from the grave fill, but all were probably redeposited.

The original form of the silver ring cannot be determined but given its location at the neck it is more likely to have been a closed band. These date from the early 6th to the 7th century and are most popular in the mid 6th century (Fisher 1979).

The amethyst pendant appears to be a failed bead as the perforations do not quite meet in the middle.

An attempt has been made using copper alloy to copy the more intricate gold settings of cabochon pendants of garnet and amethyst, well known in the 7th century. Examples include Sibertswold 172 (Faussett 1856; Hawkes and Grove 1963; Hawkes *et al.* 1966) and Standlake I 8 (Dickinson 1976). The example from Boveney was suspended on a broken copper alloy wire knot ring, and its position within the grave strongly suggests that it was broken when buried.

Wire knot rings, usually silver, are typical of 7th-century dress (Hyslop 1963, 198–9). This example is of interest as it is made of copper alloy.

Plate 3.4   Lake End Road West: Anglo-Saxon pit 41085

Plate 3.5   Lake End Road West: Anglo-Saxon pit 40581

The position of a collection of odds and ends including the amethyst pendant underneath the left pelvis suggests that they were buried in a pouch or bag. Bag collections seem to have occurred throughout the pagan Anglo-Saxon period, even into the Christian period (Ager 1989, 223). The presence of the amethyst pendant however, strongly suggests that this example is more likely to be 7th-century. Nine examples of bag collections were recorded at

Empingham II, Rutland and it was noted that they were most commonly located on the left side (Timby 1996, 60), like the example from Boveney.

A number of authors have argued that the objects within bags were kept because they possessed amuletic qualities (Brown 1972, 109; 1977, 96) or indeed, were amulets themselves. It has also been argued that miscellaneous fittings would have been kept purely because they were useful (Evison 1987,

Plate 3.6   Lake End Road East: Anglo-Saxon pit 30444

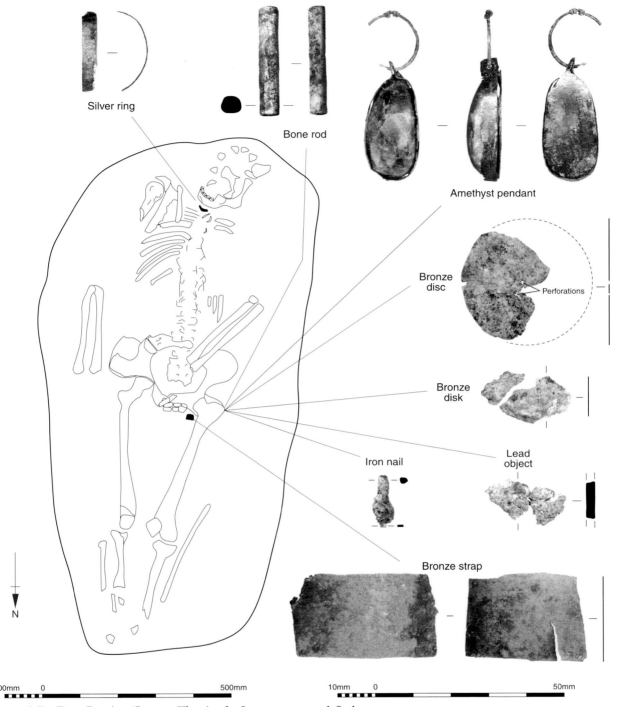

Figure 3.5 *Eton Rowing Course. The Anglo-Saxon grave and finds*

119). The evidence is inconclusive: bag collections are fairly ubiquitous and many of their contents of practical use, thus they may well have been kept for that reason, their association with amulets being purely fortuitous.

Both bag collections and finer rings have a wide period of use, but the location of the ring at the neck, probably for suspension, and the presence of the amethyst pendant, are strongly suggestive of a

7th-century date, although a late 6th-century date cannot be discounted given the radiocarbon date.

The siting of the burial (Fig. 1.4)
by Tim Allen

This burial was located 25 m east of the low-lying former channel of the Thames, and some 80 m north and west respectively of two prehistoric barrows that were probably still visible as mounds. The burial was isolated from any other Saxon activity.

The siting of Saxon burials near to earlier barrows appears to have occurred throughout the early Saxon period, beginning in the 5th century at sites such as Abingdon, Oxfordshire (Leeds and Harden 1936). In the 7th century a number of prominent Anglo-Saxons were buried under contemporary barrows in this region, most notably at the Taplow mound less than 6 km from the Boveney burial. Other examples are known at Cuddesdon and Asthall in Oxfordshire, and Lowbury in Berkshire (Blair 1994, 46–9 and fig. 38).

The association of status with barrow burial at this period is clear, and it may be that, in default of a barrow of her own, the Boveney woman was buried in the vicinity of the existing barrow group, of which the closest barrow (5169) had the deepest ditch, and probably quite a prominent mound. The practice of barrow burial, whether reusing prehistoric barrows or creating new ones, has been interpreted as part of the legitimisation of control of the land by associating the Saxon dead with the burials of the controlling lineages of the past (Wilson 1992, 70). Most of the other cited examples of this association, however, were buried either within, or at least very close to, the prehistoric burial mounds. By contrast, the Boveney burial is too far from the barrows to be confident that this association was deliberate.

It has been argued that the women buried with amuletic bag collections may have been 'wise women' who were deliberately isolated from the rest of the community in death as in life (Hinton pers. comm.). Burials of this type at Bidford and Lechlade were found on the edge of the cemeteries (Webster and Cherry 1980, 233; Boyle *et al.* 1998, 84 and Fig. 5.13), and at Orsett a burial of this type was one of an isolated pair (Hedges and Buckley 1985). This may therefore have been someone known to, but separated from a nearby Saxon community.

Chapter 4:   The Anglo-Saxon Finds and Environmental Evidence

FINDS – SUMMARY REPORTS

Full reports on the finds, including catalogues and illustrations, can be found on the CD-ROM. This volume contains summary reports and selected illustrations.

The Anglo-Saxon pottery *(Figs 4.1–2 & 5.4)*
by Paul Blinkhorn

The three excavation sites of Lake End Road West, Lot's Hole and Lake End Road East produced an interesting range of pottery. In particular, Lake End Road West is one of the growing number of middle Saxon sites from the Thames valley to produce Ipswich ware. It has also produced one of the largest assemblages of imported continental pottery outside the *wics* (see Fig. 5.4 for the distribution of imported pottery at Lake End Road West). However, despite these exotics the assemblage as a whole was dominated by early to middle Anglo-Saxon handmade wares. (Table 4.1)

A single sherd of middle Saxon pottery was recovered from Area 6 within the Eton Rowing Course study area.

The most common fabric (Fabric 1) was chaff-tempered ware. The vessels were reduced to black with reddish-brown outer surfaces and some burnishing. Wall thickness varied between 7 and 10 mm. Most of the rim sherds appear to have been from simple, globular jars with a short rim (80–280 mm), though some were slightly shouldered with hollowed-out necks. These latter examples were paralleled at Wraysbury (Astill and Lobb 1989, fig. 9, 41–3). There were also a number of more unusual forms: three vessels, from contexts 30652 (pit 30653), 40582 (pit 40581), and 41594 (pit 41593) – see Figure 4.1 nos 3 and 4 had terminal scars from longitudinal rod handles. The only parallels come from a few 5th-century vessels (Myres 1977, fig. 74; Blinkhorn 1994, 513, fig. 294.12). Three examples of hemispherical bowls were also found (Fig. 4.1 no. 5); they showed similarities to examples found at Staines (Jones and Moorhouse 1981, fig. 4 nos 1, 2). Apart from burnishing, only one vessel was decorated (Fig. 4.1 no. 2); it had a single row of thumb and finger indentations around the base of the neck.

The other common fabric was Fabric 2 a quartz-tempered ware, reduced black throughout with reddish-brown surfaces. Again, most vessels were handmade jars of simple, globular form. Three jars with plain upright rims, three with everted rims and four with rounded shoulders had parallels from amongst the assemblage at Wraysbury (Astill and Lobb 1989, fig. 9, 41–3, 46–9). One of the shouldered vessels had a smoothed exterior surface above the

shoulder, but a rough surface below (Fig. 4.2 no. 6). A more unusual form was represented by a rim fragment and a single sherd of a perforated jar or fuming pot from Lake End Road East (Fig. 4.1 no. 7).

A less common handmade ware, Fabric 3 was tempered with calcareous gravel, and like the others, reduced to black throughout with reddish brown surfaces. Only two hand-built jars were recovered: one at Lot's Hole with a thickened inturned rim and one at Lake End Road West (Fig. 4.1 no. 8). A quartz- and organic-tempered ware (Fabric 4) was found at Lake End Road East, where it was represented by two flat bases, probably from jars similar to those from Wraysbury (Astill and Lobb 1989, fig. 9, 54), a rim from a plain upright jar (Fig. 4.1 no. 9) and a group of decorated, stabbed and grooved sherds from the same vessel (Fig. 4.1 no. 10). A single sherd of the same fabric was also recovered from Lot's Hole. A single, unusual grog-tempered pitcher (Fabric 5) was noted at Lake End Road West; parallels are known from London and Southampton with a broad middle Saxon to Late Saxon/Norman date (Blackmore 1988, 88; Timby 1988, 90).

These five fabrics probably all had their origin in the local area, but pottery was clearly also arriving at the site from further afield. Three sherds of Ipswich ware were recovered from Lake End Road West, a rare find outside East Anglia. This is a middle Saxon slow-wheel made ware, manufactured exclusively in Ipswich. Outside East Anglia Ipswich Ware is mainly dated to AD 725–40-early/mid 9th century.

There were also imports from outside Britain. A variety of sand-tempered, wheel-thrown North French wares was found, including rims and the handle of a pitcher (Fig. 4.2 nos 11 & 13). More unusually three sherds of Tating ware from the Rhineland were also recovered from Lake End Road West (Fig. 4.2 no. 12 & Pl. 4.1).

Gravel Storage Area

Fourteen sherds of early to middle Saxon pottery were recovered from the stripped area and the eleven test pits. The most common wares were from six hand-built jars tempered with coarse organic chaff (Fabric 1). A similar ware occurred at all three excavation sites.

The metalwork *(Figs 4.3–6)*
by Ian Scott

The metalwork assemblage from the sites mainly consists of iron objects though a few copper alloy objects and some lead scrap were also found. Four copper alloy pins of typical middle Saxon forms,

Table 4.1   All pottery quantities, types and fabrics and periods from the three main sites of the Flood Alleviation Scheme

Period and Fabric Type (F)	Site Name									Total Per Fabric Type		
(I) EARLY MEDIEVAL	Lake End Road West			Lake End Road East			Lot's Hole					
1. Early to Middle Saxon	EVEs	Sh	Wt	EVEs	Sh	Wt	EVEs	Sh	Wt	EVEs	Sh	Wt
F1 Chaff	6.67	414	8087	0.72	35	624	2.25	182	2658	9.64	631	10966
F2 Quartz black warp	2.37	252	5517	0.35	60	649	0.25	39	230	2.97	351	6396
F3 Calcareous	0.65	24	909	0	2	30	0	1	20	0.65	27	959
F4 Quartz and Organic	–	–	–	0.05	20	592	0	1	4	0.05	21	596
F5 Grog tempered	0.23	4	470	–	–	–	–	–	–	0.23	4	470
F6 Quartz grey ware	0	2	25	–	–	–	–	–	–	0	2	25
TOTALS FOR E-M SAXON	9.92	696	15008	1.12	117	1895	2.5	223	2912	13.54	1036	19815
2. Middle to late Saxon												
F7 Ipswich Ware	0	3	70	–	–	–	–	–	–	0	3	70
F8 Continental Wares	0.23	18	506	–	–	–	–	–	–	0.23	18	506
TOTALS FOR M-L SAXON	0.23	21	576	–	–	–	–	–	–	0.23	21	576
3. Late Saxon & Saxo Norman												
F9 Calcareous	–	–	–	–	–	–	1.1	67	850	1.1	67	850
F10 Shell	–	–	–	–	–	–	0.4	16	454	0.4	16	454
F11 Coarse Shell	–	–	–	0	1	8	–	–	–	0	1	8
F12 Chalk	–	–	–	–	–	–	0	5	22	0	5	22
F13 St Neots	–	–	–	–	–	–	0.05	31	152	0.05	31	152
F14 Saxo-Norman	–	–	–	0.5	46	530	0.05	7	66	0.55	53	596
F15 Quartz, Flint, Chalk & Grog	–	–	–	0	22	326	0.7	96	1104	0.7	118	1430
TOTALS FOR LS & S Norm.	–	–	–	0.5	69	864	2.3	222	2648	2.8	291	3512
(II) MEDIEVAL												
1. Possible Earlier Wares												
F16 Quartz, iron-rich	–	–	–	0	1	10	0.45	38	428	0.45	39	438
F17 E.Wilts, qu & flint	–	–	–	–	–	–	1.2	126	1442	1.2	126	1442
F18 Quartz-Grey	–	–·	–	3.05	360	5000	6.8	1183	12958	9.85	1543	17958
TOTALS FOR Earl. Med.Wa												
2. Medieval Wares												
F19 Local Oxidised	–	–	–	0.30	26	306	0.25	15	210	0.55	41	516
F20 Coarse London	–	–	–	0	7	142	0	3	62	0	10	24
F21 London type	–	–	–	0	1	130	0	2	18	0	3	148
F22 Kingston type	–	–	–	0.1	83	944	0	23	270	0.1	106	1214
F23 Cheam whiteware	–	–	–	0	7	48	0	1	2	0	8	50
F24 Coarse Border	–	–	–	0.3	33	276	0	10	72	0.3	43	348
F25 Tudor Green	–	–	–	0	2	4	–	–	–	0	2	4
TOTALS FOR MEDIEVAL	–	–	–	0.7	159	1850	0.25	54	634	0.95	213	2484
(III) POST-MEDIEVAL												
1. European Imports												
F26 Raeren/ Aachen Stoneware	–	–	–	0	6	114	–	–	–	0	6	114
F27 Cologue/ Frechen Stoneware	–	–	–	0	1	38	–	–	–	0	1	38
F28 Westerwald Stoneware	–	–	–	0	1	10	–	–	–	0	1	10
2. Others												
F29 Brill/Boarstal	–	–	–	0	5	60	–	–	–	0	5	60
F30 Tudor Brown Earthenware	–	–	–	0.55	4	102	–	–	–	0.55	4	102
F31 Tudor Red Earthenware	–	–	–	0.20	12	112	–	–	–	1.20	12	112
F32 Fine Red Earthenware	–	–	–	2.95	295	5842	0	2	10	2.95	297	5852
F33 Coarse Red Earthenware	–	–	–	0	19	356	–	–	–	0	19	356
F34 Blackware	–	–	–	0	5	26	–	–	–	0	5	26
F35 Slipware	–	–	–	0	3	50	–	–	–	0	3	50

Table 4.1 *(Continued)*

Period and Fabric Type (F)	Site Name									Total Per Fabric Type		
(III) POST-MEDIEVAL	Lake End Road West			Lake End Road East			Lot's Hole					
F36 Border Ware	–	–	–	0.25	60	932	–	–	–	0.25	60	932
F37 Others Later jars, Tinglaze, 18th Staffs, Eng. Porcelain, Creamware, Transfer printed ware,												
TOTALS FOR POST-MED	–	–	–	4.05	419	7672	0	5	20	4.05	424	7692
TOTALS FOR ALL TYPES	10.5	717	15584	9.42	1125	17291	13.5	1851	21042	16.73	3693	53917

Abbreviations used in this section:

F = Fabric Type

EVEs = Estimated Vessel Equivalent

Sh = No of Sherds

Wt = Weight in grams

paralleled at *Hamwic,* were recovered; three from Lake End Road West and one from Lot's Hole (Fig. 4.3 nos 2, 3, 4 & 5). A few small scraps of copper wire also came from Saxon contexts at Lot's Hole and Lake End Road West. An unstratified pair of tweezers from Lake End Road West is also probably of Anglo-Saxon date (Fig. 4.3 no. 1 & Pl. 4.2) and one small piece of casting waste from the same site suggests that some copper alloy working may have taken place on the site.

The ironwork assemblage was equally undistinguished. A few personal objects were recognised from Lake End Road West, including a possible pin and two strap-ends. One was shaped like a small spearhead and retained traces of tinning or silvering around the attachment and at the junction of the blade and socket. The other was simpler in form consisting of a simple bar of square section with a flattened and divided end; it also retained traces of tinning or silvering.

A number of lock and key fragments were found at Lake End Road West. A T-shaped lift-key and a barb-spring padlock bolt were found (Fig. 4.4 nos 1 & 3), as well as two possible fragments from a barb-spring padlock, and a possible padlock case (Fig. 4.4 no. 2). A badly corroded bucket handle, was found at Lake End Road East, formed from a rod bent into a semi-circle which had a decorative inlay of five chevrons or zigzags of non-ferrous metal on its outer face, adjacent to the hand grip (Fig. 4.5 no. 4; the zigzag decoration is visible on Pl. 4.3).

A total of 17 heckle teeth fragments were found, all from Lake End Road West, in addition to a heckle- or wool- comb fragment comprising 13 teeth set in a wood block with iron binding (Fig. 4.5 no. 5). Other iron objects included tools, such as a chisel/punch and an awl (Fig. 4.5 no. 6) from Lake End Road West, as well as possible fragments of bells and a chain link from Lake End Road East.

Knives were the most common iron implement; 20 complete or fragmentary knives were found at Lake End Road West, and examples were also found at both Lot's Hole and Lake End Road East (Fig. 4.6).

Other groups of objects included a number of lead strips and offcuts that were found in spoil and in Anglo-Saxon contexts at Lot's Hole, as well as several fragments of melted waste. No definable objects were recognised, but some of the rolled strips of sheeting could have been used as net sinkers.

Numerically the whole iron assemblage was dominated by iron nails, though many may have been of later medieval rather than Saxon date: of the 64 nails from Lake End Road East only one was from an Anglo-Saxon context.

The worked stone *(Fig. 4.7)*
by Fiona Roe

The main characteristic of this stone assemblage is the quantity of Niedermendig lava from the Rhineland, which was found on all three sites (Lake End Road West, Lake End Road East and Lot's Hole). Altogether 45 pits of middle Saxon date produced fragments of lava, amounting to some 13 kg. Among this assemblage was a large fragment of rotary quern, with traces of a raised collar round the central hole (Fig. 4.7 no. 1). Otherwise the lava finds are nearly all very fragmentary, averaging only 288 g per pit, but they nevertheless suggest that large numbers of lava querns were being brought to the area from about the 6th to 8th centuries AD. Further finds from Lake End Road East and Lot's Hole demonstrate that the lava continued to arrive in this country during the late Saxon, medieval and post-medieval periods.

Other corn-grinding materials were used in altogether smaller quantities. Triassic sandstone, possibly also from Germany, was used for a small millstone. There are 12 fragments of Greensand from Surrey, recorded both from middle Saxon and post- medieval contexts, while four pieces of Millstone Grit are from contexts of varied periods. Some quern fragments

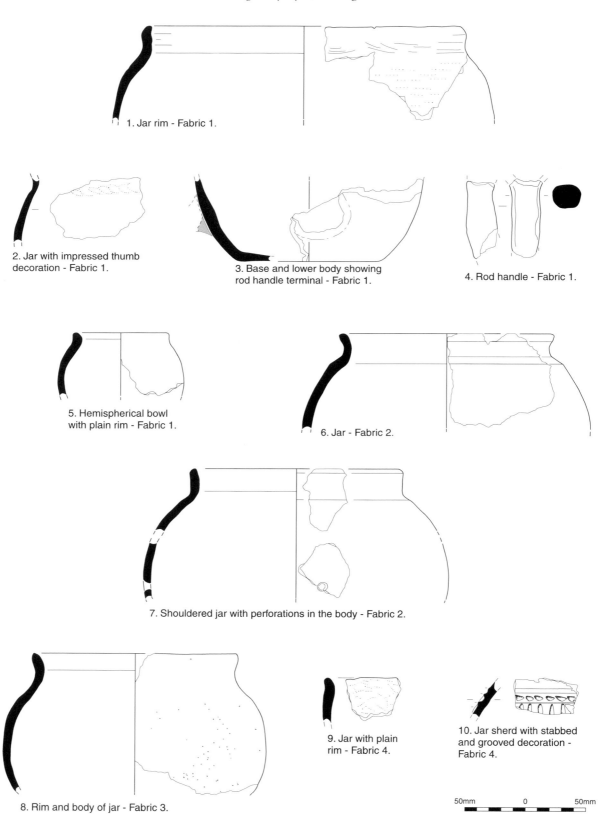

1. Jar rim - Fabric 1.

2. Jar with impressed thumb decoration - Fabric 1.

3. Base and lower body showing rod handle terminal - Fabric 1.

4. Rod handle - Fabric 1.

5. Hemispherical bowl with plain rim - Fabric 1.

6. Jar - Fabric 2.

7. Shouldered jar with perforations in the body - Fabric 2.

8. Rim and body of jar - Fabric 3.

9. Jar with plain rim - Fabric 4.

10. Jar sherd with stabbed and grooved decoration - Fabric 4.

50mm   0   50mm

Figure 4.1   *Anglo-Saxon pottery 1–10, local handmade pottery*

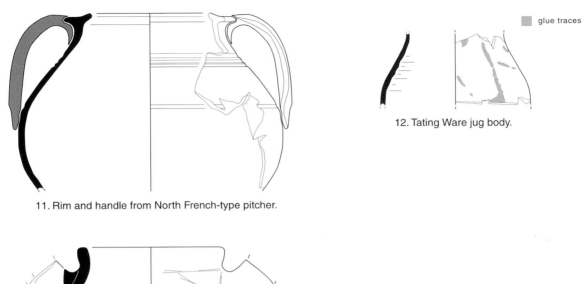

11. Rim and handle from North French-type pitcher.

12. Tating Ware jug body.

glue traces

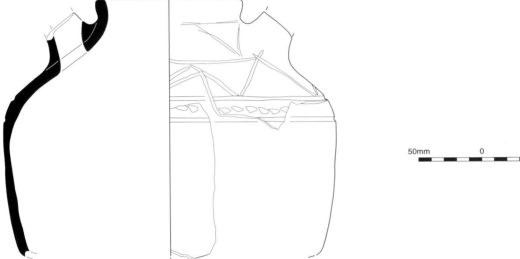

13. Rim, spout and upper body of large pitcher.

50mm 0 50mm

Figure 4.2 *Anglo-Saxon pottery 11–13, imported wares*

may be redeposited Roman material, particularly those made from Old Red Sandstone and Lodsworth Greensand, and probably also the pieces of Millstone Grit. A few fragments seem more likely to belong with earlier prehistoric material, as do most of the pieces of burnt stone. This extraneous material will be discussed in more detail in Volumes 1 and 2.

All seven whetstones from the excavations came from Saxon pits at Lake End Road West. Two of these (context 41671, pit 41593, SF 42536 and context 41285, pit 41328, SF 42188 – Fig. 4.7 no. 2) appear to be made from Lower Calcareous Grit. This is another material which was imported to the site, since it is an Upper Jurassic calcareous sandstone, that occurs in the Corallian of Oxfordshire, in particular around Cumnor and Marcham (Arkell 1939). The remaining whetstones are made from medium to fine-grained sandstones, at least two of which are likely to have been collected from local river gravels. There is also the possibility that one or two may have been imported from the continent, along with the querns.

There is one stone spindlewhorl, plano-convex in shape and made from Greensand, now burnt (context 40405, pit 40356, SF 42795, Fig. 4.7 no. 3). Another small object is a fragment from a possible rubber made from Jurassic limestone (context 41377, pit 41376, SF 42516).

The bone and antler objects *(Figs 4.8–10)*
by Ian Riddler

A total of 39 middle Saxon bone and antler objects were recovered from the sites. The assemblage includes a dress pin, 19 combs, 8 pin-beaters, 4 needles, 2 modified pig fibulae and a possible bow guard (Pl. 4.5).

Nineteen combs were recovered from seventeen separate pit fills, mainly from Lake End Road West. Eighteen are double-sided composite combs, while one has a handle. None of the combs are complete and it is only possible to reconstruct the length of two of them. However, on the basis of width it is possible to divide them into two groups. Five combs

Plate 4.1   *Reconstruction of Tating Ware vessel*

belong in the broader group (>35 mm) (see Fig. 4.8 nos 1 & 2). Parallels can be found for combs within this group from a range of sites, including Dorchester (Sparey-Green 1984, fig. 13.10), York (Rogers 1993, fig. 683.5739) and Canterbury. Most can best be understood in a later 7th- or 8th-century context, though one with a connecting plate decorated with a chequer-board pattern (SF 42888 Fig. 4.8 no. 2) may belong to a slightly later period.

The narrower combs (see Fig. 4.8 nos 3 & 4) also have parallels from the same range of sites, where they tend to date slightly later; they are very rare in the 7th century and not common until after *c* 750. This suggests that as a whole most of the assemblage belongs to the early/mid 8th century. The exceptions are one comb mentioned above (SF 42888) and the handled comb (Fig. 4.9 no. 5 & Pl. 4.4), both of which may belong to the 9th/10th

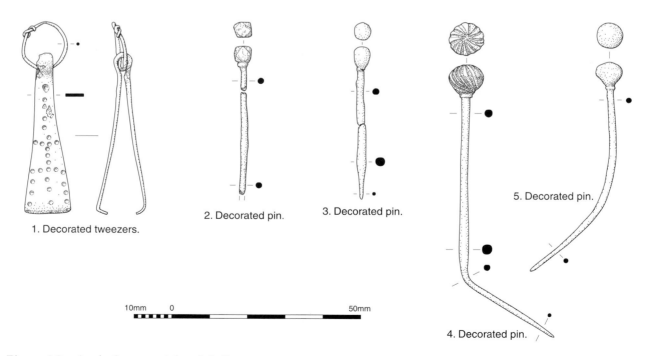

1. Decorated tweezers.

2. Decorated pin.

3. Decorated pin.

4. Decorated pin.

5. Decorated pin.

10mm   0   50mm

Figure 4.3   *Anglo-Saxon metalwork 1–5*

40

Plate 4.2   *Bronze tweezers*

centuries. Combs with perforated handles were widespread in Anglo-Saxon England during the 9th and 10th centuries although few come from well-dated contexts. The various elements of decoration of the comb are familiar across the type as a whole, bands of fret pattern occurring frequently on handled combs from the 8th century onwards. The raised end of the Lake End Road West comb is a feature paralleled by a comb of the same type from Canterbury (Blockley *et al.* 1995, fig. 513.1174). Although raised ends suggest a 10th century date, the practice may possibly have its origins in the later 9th century.

An unusual object of antler (Fig. 4.9 no. 6 & Pl. 4.5) is decorated on one side by a panel of repeated curvilinear designs within a frame formed from a single bounding line. The pattern consists in each case of two curves and two oblique lines with pecked decorations applied across all the available space. Similar artefacts, decorated on one face, are known from *Hamwic*, York and possibly London (Holdsworth 1980, fig. 15.1.6; Rogers 1993, fig. 686.5609; Waterman 1959, pl. XX.2; Whytehead and Blackmore 1988, fig. 38.12). All are probably of middle Saxon date, though the York example may be later. It has been suggested that these objects might act as bow guards, worn on the inside of the wrist and secured with thongs which were passed through the transverse slots (Underwood 1998).

The dress pin (Fig. 4.10 no. 7) was made from a pig fibula with a squared head and a central circular perforation. The shape of the head would have prevented it from passing through fabric and it is likely on this basis to have served as a dress pin rather than a needle; parallels are known from Birka, Ipswich, North Elmham and York (Schwarz-Mack-

ensen 1976, 35–7; Riddler, Trzaska and Hatton forthcoming; Wade-Martins 1980, fig. 20.21; MacGregor 1982, fig. 48.504; MacGregor, Mainman and Rogers 1999, fig. 909.6851).

A small number of bone textile implements were also found, including both pin-beaters and needles (Fig. 4.10 nos 8–11). The needles are made from pig fibulae and occur in a variety of head shapes; all the pin-beaters are of double-pointed form, which is usually associated with a warp-weighted loom. The function of some of the other objects is less certain. It is not possible to date either pin beaters or needles with any precision, but there are some indications that the assemblage dates to the middle Saxon period.

The fired clay objects (Fig. 4.11 & Pl. 4.6)
by Kayt Brown and Nigel Jeffries

The fired clay assemblage includes 237 fragmentary loomweights and a spindlewhorl. The material was recovered from pit fills and general soil horizons. Of these 29 loomweights were characterised according to Hurst's classification of annular, intermediate and bun-shaped loomweights (1959). Within this classification, if the central hole is the same width or wider than the surrounding clay ring it is annular; if the central hole is less than the width of the clay ring it is intermediate. Where the hole is much smaller and pierced, it is bun-shaped (Hurst 1959, 23–4). These loomweight types also follow a general chronology proceeding from annular (early Saxon) through intermediate (middle Saxon, of which there were 22 here) to bun-shaped loomweights (of which there were 7 here), which are generally considered to be later Saxon (ibid. 24). Given the small number that were identifiable to type, the apparent absence of

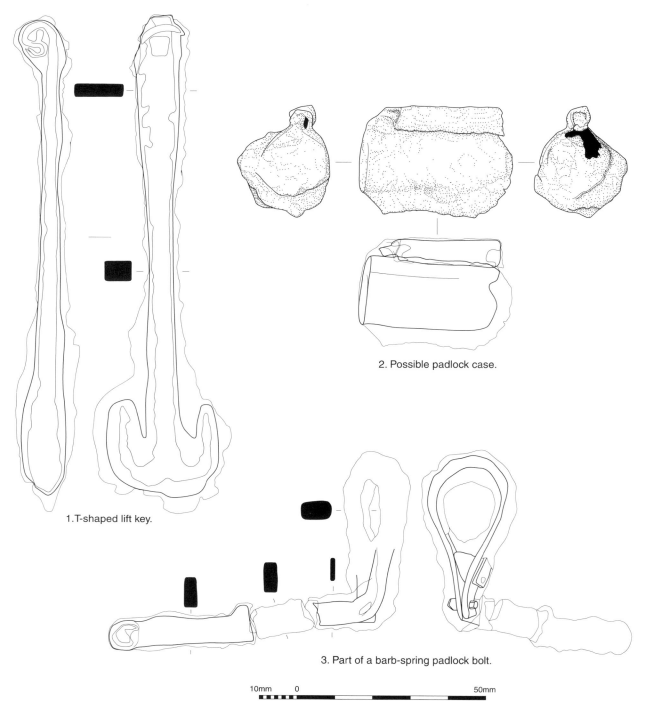

1.T-shaped lift key.

2. Possible padlock case.

3. Part of a barb-spring padlock bolt.

10mm   0   50mm

Figure 4.4   *Anglo-Saxon ironwork 1–3*

annular loomweights may be a consequence of artefact survival.

The burnt clay
by Kayt Brown

A total of 4099 fragments of burnt clay, weighing 41,454 g, was recovered from Saxon (and later) contexts at Lake End Road West (2536 fragments, 27,848 g) and Lake End Road East (387 fragments, 4002 g), and from medieval contexts at Lot's Hole (1230 fragments, 10,907 g). The material from Lake End Road West includes fragments recovered during the processing of samples taken for environmental sampling. The fabrics corresponded with those identified for the loomweights. Details of the quantities and fabric types are included in the Burnt Clay section of the CD-ROM.

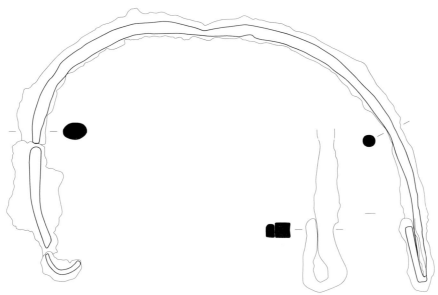

4. Bucket handle with traces of inlaid decoration (see Plate 4.3).

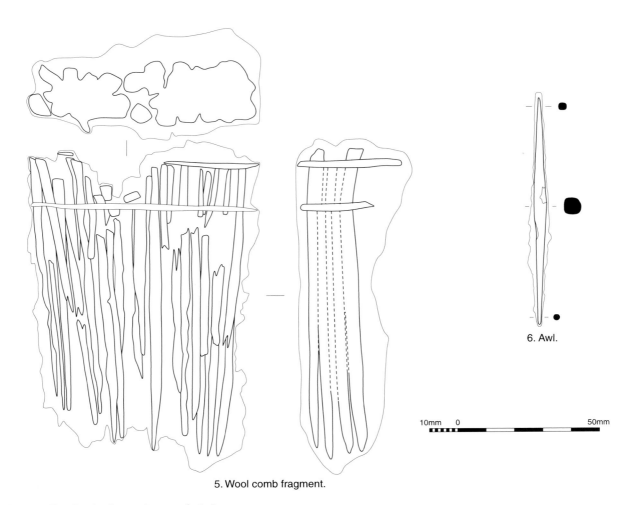

5. Wool comb fragment.

6. Awl.

10mm　0　　　　　　　　　　　50mm

Figure 4.5　*Anglo-Saxon ironwork 4–6*

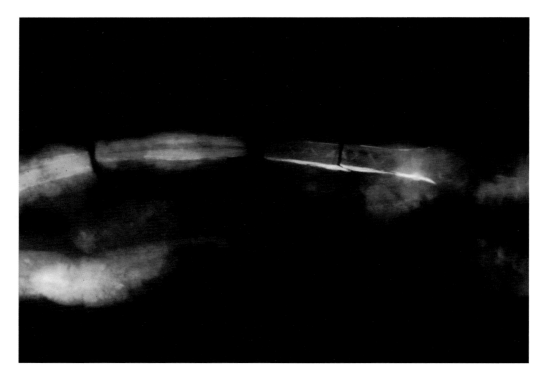

Plate 4.3   *X-ray of iron bucket-handle with non-ferrous metal inlay*

The majority of the burnt clay comprised amorphous lumps of material that could not be assigned a function, but fragments displayed flat surfaces and may represent linings from hearths or other structures. For example, at Lake End Road West a number of fragments had charcoal adhering to one surface and vitrified clay lining was also recovered. Three fragments from Lake End Road East had what appeared to be a layer of limescale on the surface. Possible daub was recovered from all three sites, although because of the fragmentary nature of much of the assemblage it can only be identified as structural (it displays smoothed surfaces but no wattle impressions were observed) or amorphous pieces. Burnt clay is a common find on sites of this period resulting from a range of domestic activities and is often found scattered across the site, as is the case at these three sites where the burnt clay was recovered from a range of feature fills and layers.

The glass (*Fig. 4.12 & Pl. 4.7*)
by Cecily Cropper

Three fragments of Anglo-Saxon glass were recovered. A rim of a green-tinted palm cup of 6th–8th century date (Fig. 4.12 no. 1) and a fragment of mould-blown vessel of 8th–9th century date (Fig. 4.12 no. 2) were found at Lot's Hole. A rim fragment, from a palm cup or funnel beaker, decorated with horizontal, white, marvered trails came from Lake End Road West (Fig. 4.12 no. 3 & Pl. 4.7), and can be compared directly with examples from Hamwic, fitting into the later part of the palm cup/funnel beaker sequence as identified by Hunter (1980, fig. 11, 3, no. 4, GL.5).

The iron slag
by Lyn Keyes

An assemblage of iron slag weighing 46.2 kg was recovered from the Saxon contexts from Lake End Road West. The bulk of this material represents secondary smithing, that is, the hot working of an iron shape by a smith to turn it into a utilitarian object. There was no evidence here for smelting, which is the primary manufacture of iron from ore and a flux, although a very small amount of un-diagnostic slag was found (2 kg). Almost 37 kg of the total amount of slag comprised smithing hearth bottoms; 5.3 kg of smithing slag lumps was also recovered. The distribution of metalworking waste is considered in the discussion (Chapter 5) and displayed in Figure 5.5.

ECOFACTUAL AND ENVIRONMENTAL EVIDENCE – SUMMARY REPORTS

Full reports on the environmental evidence, including tables and figures, can be found on the CD-ROM.

The animal bone (*Fig. 4.13*)
by Adrienne Powell

The bone assemblages yield a total of 18,769 fragments, comprising 1294 fragments from Lot's Hole and 17,475 from Lake End Road, with an overall level of identification of 28%. Most of the identified bone in both assemblages is from the domestic mammals but this proportion is higher at Lot's Hole

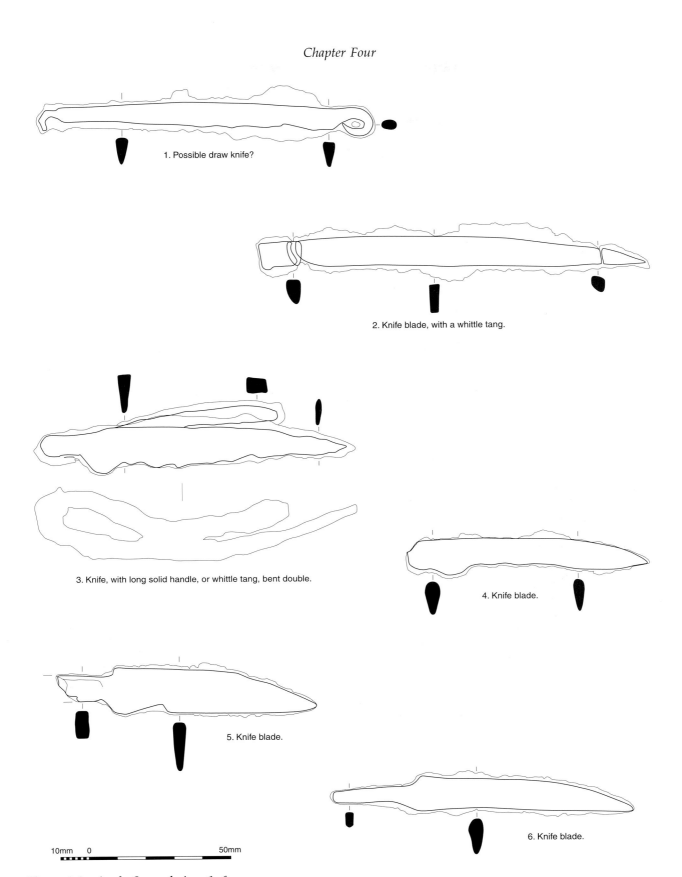

1. Possible draw knife?

2. Knife blade, with a whittle tang.

3. Knife, with long solid handle, or whittle tang, bent double.

4. Knife blade.

5. Knife blade.

6. Knife blade.

10mm 0   50mm

Figure 4.6   *Anglo-Saxon knives 1–6*

(94%) than at Lake End Road (88%). In both assemblages cattle remains are predominant but at Lake End Road West they are followed in frequency by pig bones, whereas at Lot's Hole caprine bones are the next most frequent. Only four goat bones were identified in these assemblages: one distal humerus

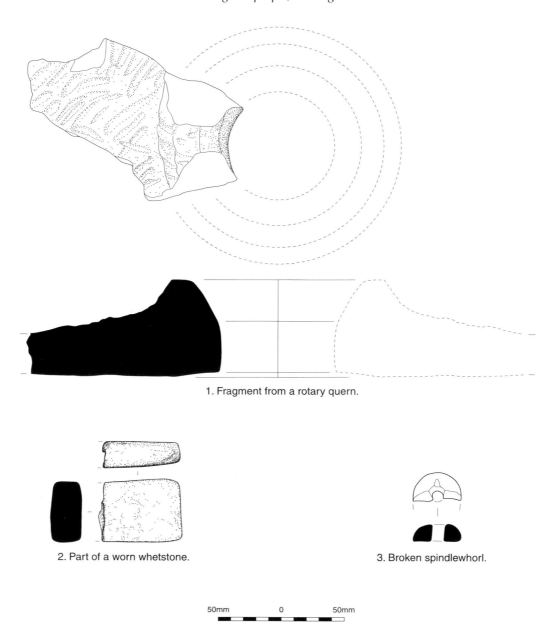

1. Fragment from a rotary quern.

2. Part of a worn whetstone.

3. Broken spindlewhorl.

50mm   0   50mm

Figure 4.7   *Anglo-Saxon worked stone 1–3*

from Lot's Hole and two horn cores and one distal tibia from Lake End Road. Approximately 15% of the remaining caprine bones are sheep, so it is likely that most of the undifferentiated material is also sheep. Cattle would probably have provided most of the meat in the diet, even although it was not the most common in terms of individual animals. Pig, as pork, ham or bacon, would have been the next most important. Horse and dog bones are present in both assemblages as minor components but cat is rarer still and only occurs at Lake End Road.

Several wild mammal species occur in the Lake End Road assemblage of which deer, especially roe deer (*Capreolus capreolus*), are the most common. Only wild boar (*Sus scrofa*) occurs in the Lot's Hole assemblage. Bird bones comprise a relatively large proportion of the identifiable bone at Lake End Road but are less frequent at Lot's Hole. Domestic fowl is the most common species in both assemblages but a small range of wildfowl is also present. Herpetofauna and fish are only represented in small numbers.

The importance of cattle is typical of contemporary sites, as can be seen in Figure 4.13, where the relative contributions (percentage number of identified species (NISP)) of the three main domestic mammals are compared. The low percentage of sheep and high percentage of pigs is worth noting, and is comparable to some other sites, although not necessarily for the same reasons. The only sites where sheep are as rare as at Lake End Road and pigs similarly frequent are Maiden Lane, London (West 1988), Brimpton (Cram 1986–90), which has a

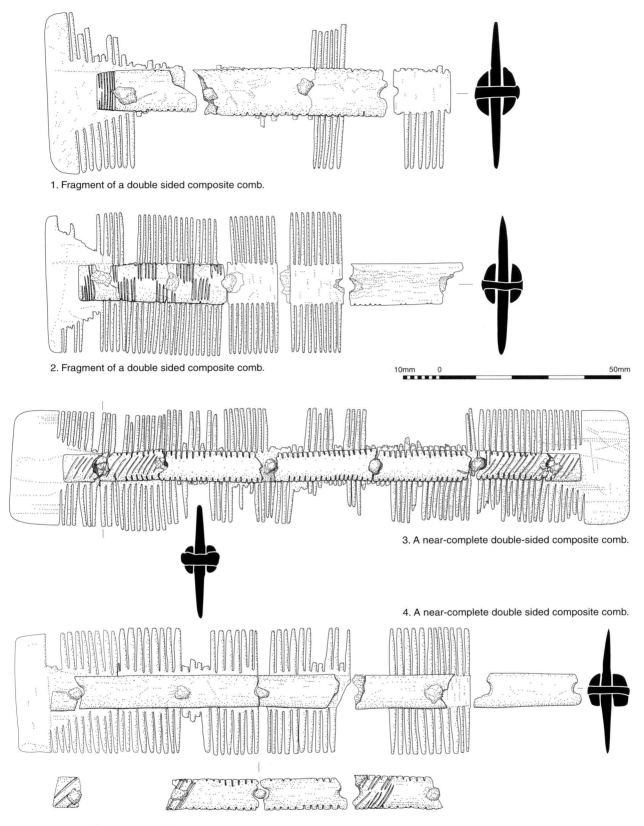

1. Fragment of a double sided composite comb.

2. Fragment of a double sided composite comb.

3. A near-complete double-sided composite comb.

4. A near-complete double sided composite comb.

Figure 4.8   *Anglo-Saxon combs 1–4*

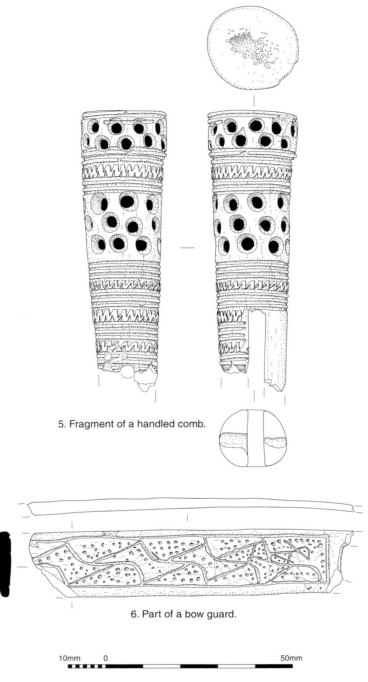

5. Fragment of a handled comb.

6. Part of a bow guard.

10mm 0 50mm

Figure 4.9   *Anglo-Saxon worked bone and antler (objects) 5–6*

very small sample size, and Wicken Bonhunt (Crabtree 1996) which appears to be a specialist pig breeding centre. The pattern is also present although less marked at sites such as Ipswich (Crabtree 1996), the London Peabody site (West 1989), Wraysbury (Coy 1987), Ramsbury (Coy 1980) and the Jubilee Hall site, London (West 1988).

The age profiles of the three main domestic species, with the scarcity of very young cattle, sheep and pig and of skeletally mature cattle and sheep – consumption of both immature and adult pigs having

been practised by the Saxons (Hagen 1995) – are consistent with a consumer site rather than a producer site. The animals represented are mainly of prime age for culling for meat, allowing for constraints of a non-intensive husbandry regime. For example, the scarcity of cattle with M_3s in the early stages of wear indicates the absence of traction beasts and productive milch cows, animals too important to slaughter for meat until their productivity declines.

The representation of body parts for the main species shows that many, if not most, of the

Plate 4.4 *Bone comb handle*

animals arrived on site on the hoof although the imbalance between pig fore and hind limb elements suggests that some pork arrived as joints. The butchery evidence indicates that all stages of carcass processing occurred here, from skinning to marrow extraction. Marks on cattle horn cores indicate removal of the horn sheaths for working, but whether more than the initial removal was carried out on this site is impossible to say. These activities do not appear to have been carried out on a systematic basis since none of the pits had contents characteristic of dumps of primary butchery or industrial waste.

The charred plant remains
by Ruth Pelling

A total of 25 environmental samples were selected for full analysis following the post-excavation assessment: 21 samples were analysed from Lake End Road (West and East), and four from Lot's Hole. All of the samples were from pit fills, broadly of middle Saxon date. The assemblage comprises a wide range of cereal remains and provides evidence of processed crops; the possible use of grain for fuel, and other food types including legumes; weed seeds were common.

At Lot's Hole cereal grain was the dominant component (61%) of which wheat forms the greatest proportion. Free-threshing grain dominates but there is some hulled wheat. Barley is also present as a major cereal, with oats and rye present as minor components. Chaff and weeds are present in equal amounts (each forming 18% of total assemblage); occasional legumes and flax seeds were also identified. The chaff element includes frequent free-threshing wheat rachis; rye rachis was also present with some barley.

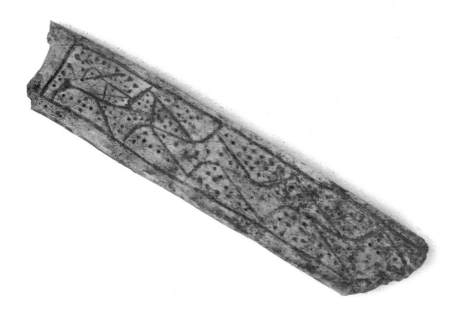

Plate 4.5 *Bow guard made of antler*

49

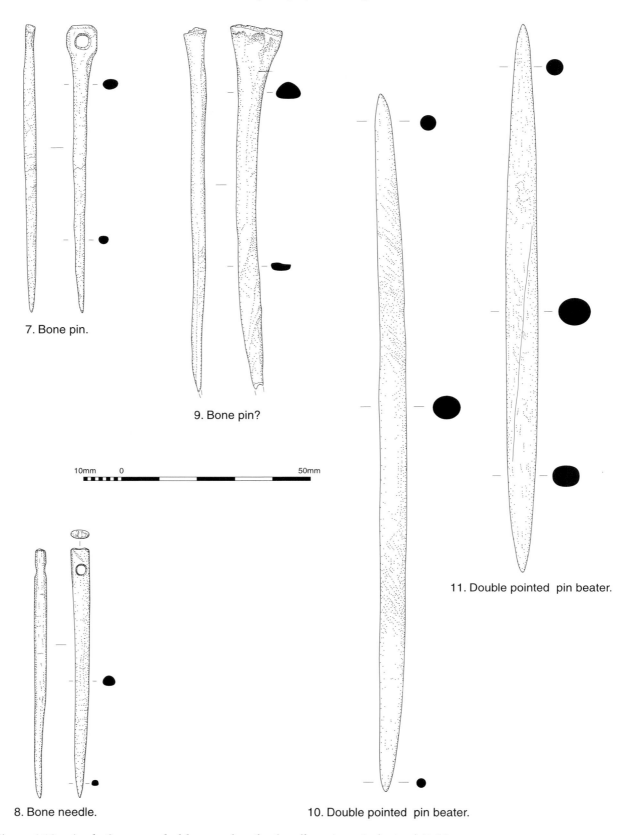

7. Bone pin.

9. Bone pin?

10mm 0 50mm

11. Double pointed pin beater.

8. Bone needle.

10. Double pointed pin beater.

Figure 4.10   *Anglo-Saxon worked bone and antler (needles, pins, pin-beaters) 7–11*

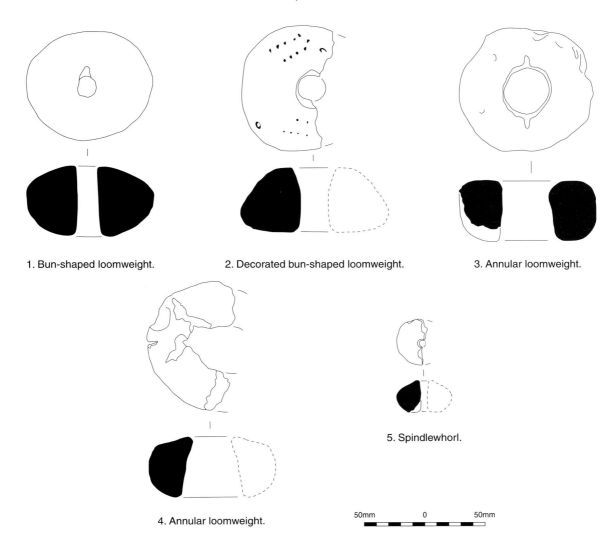

1. Bun-shaped loomweight.

2. Decorated bun-shaped loomweight.

3. Annular loomweight.

4. Annular loomweight.

5. Spindlewhorl.

50mm   0   50mm

Figure 4.11   *Anglo-Saxon loomweights 1–4, spindlewhorl 5*

Plate 4.6 Loomweights and bone textile making implements

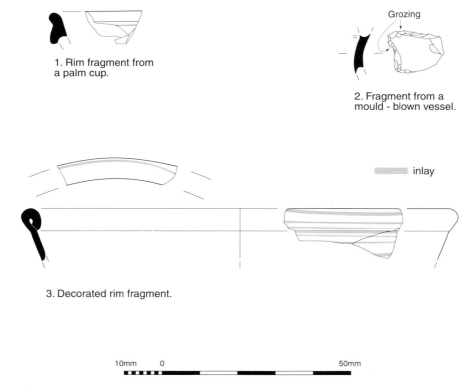

1. Rim fragment from a palm cup.

Grozing

2. Fragment from a mould - blown vessel.

inlay

3. Decorated rim fragment.

10mm   0   50mm

Figure 4.12   *Anglo-Saxon glass 1–3*

At Lake End Road East weed seeds dominated (68% of total). Grain formed 20% of the assemblage while chaff formed only 4%. Wheat was the most commonly identified cereal, forming 32% of the total grain. Barley occurs in similar numbers to wheat in five features, forming 20% overall. Oats were present in small numbers and occasional rye was identified on the basis of its rachis.

At Lake End Road West weeds were dominant (49%); grain formed 30% and chaff formed 20.5%.

Concentrations of chaff were found in several pits. Weed seeds dominated the samples in some features (Pits 40356, 40697), but were present in similar amounts to grain in the other samples. Barley grain was slightly more common than wheat (24–30%) and oats and rye form minor components (9%; 6% respectively).

Of the identifiable cereals, wheat seems to be slightly more common at Lot's Hole and Lake End Road East. The Lake End Road West samples may

Plate 4.7   *Anglo-Saxon vessel glass*

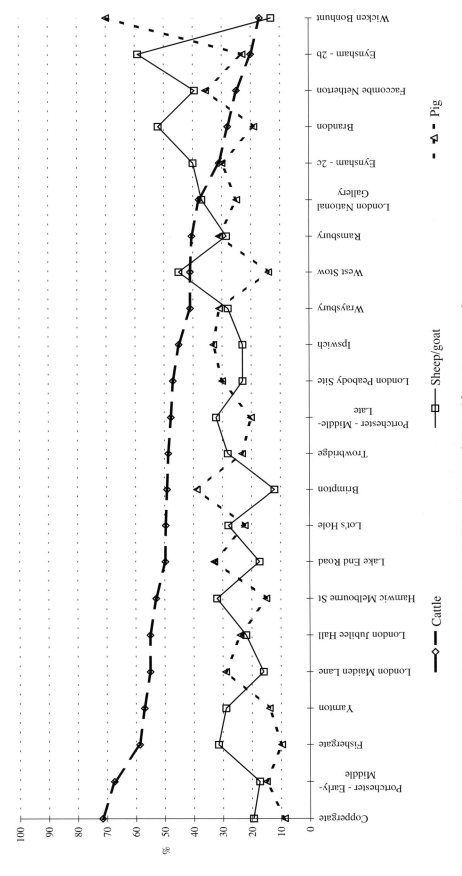

Figure 4.13   Comparison of main species proportions at Lake End Road West and East with contemporary sites

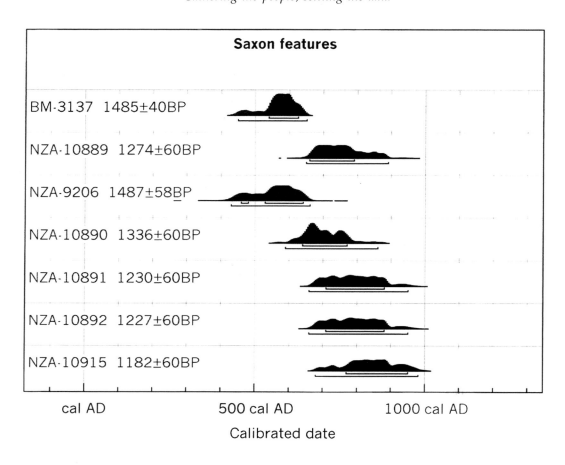

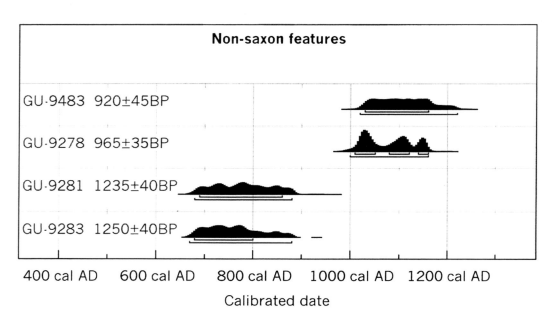

Figure 4.14 Radiocarbon dates from Saxon and non-Saxon features

give a better indicator, however, given the larger sizes of the assemblages, and here barley is most frequently identified. Oats occur at all three sites. Rye is a minor element at Lot's Hole and Lake End Road East (mostly represented by rachis), but is quite frequent at Lake End Road West.

One pit (40356) contained grain and glume bases of emmer wheat. Occasional emmer and spelt wheat glume base are recorded at Saxon sites in southern England, though they are usually interpreted as either residual contaminants deriving from Roman or prehistoric deposits or weeds of other crops. However this evidence from Lake End Road West and also Worton Rectory Farm, Yarnton (M. Robinson pers. comm.) suggests that some emmer must have been cultivated as a crop in the post-Roman period in the middle and Upper Thames Valley.

Occasional seeds and capsule fragments of flax (*Linum usitutissimum*) were present in several samples, while a large deposit of charred flax capsules was recovered from one Lake End Road East sample (30589). The presence of large quantities of capsule fragments appears to indicate that the seeds were the result of beating or combing the flax to remove the seeds prior to processing for cloth.

Radiocarbon dating (Fig. 4.14)
by Dawn Chambers

A total of 11 radiocarbon dated samples produced Saxon dates. Seven radiocarbon determinations were obtained for features of Saxon date, while the dating of a further four samples from prehistoric features also produced Saxon dates. Six dates were undertaken by the Rafter Radiocarbon Laboratory, New Zealand, four by the Scottish Universities Research and Reactor Centre and one by the British Museum. Details of all dates are tabulated on the CD-ROM and are displayed in Figure 4.14 here.

In the first instance six dates were obtained, five on animal bone and one on charred plant remains,

all from Saxon pit deposits. One context was chosen from Lot's Hole, the remainder from Lake End Road West. The animal bones were selected from pits that were thought to be of broad middle Saxon date by association with pottery and other finds. One bone sample was selected from the excavations at Lot's Hole, the other samples were from pits at Lake End Road West. The results from the samples appear to complement the ceramic and other artefactual evidence: all of the samples fall within the period cal AD 600–990 and approximate to what is defined as the middle Saxon period. However, the fifth date (NZA-9206) on charred wheat is somewhat earlier (cal AD 430–660) than the other results from the Saxon pits.

One radiocarbon date (BM-3137) was produced from the skeleton of the middle Saxon burial found at the Eton Rowing Course (see Chapter 3). This date is almost identical to that obtained from the charred wheat at Lake End Road West. Three other sampled pit deposits from Lake End Road West and one posthole deposit from Lot's Hole, otherwise undated and initially thought to be prehistoric, produced middle Saxon and Sax-Norman dates.

Other environmental analyses

Small-scale analyses were carried out on samples recovered from pit fills to investigate the presence of phytoliths (by Martin Hodson) and pollen (by Adrian Parker), and the soil micromorphology and chemistry (Richard McPhail). The full reports of these investigations can be found in the appropriate section on the CD-ROM.

Chapter 5:   Discussion of the Anglo-Saxon Archaeology

by Jonathan Hiller, David Petts and Tim Allen

The Anglo-Saxon archaeology was overwhelmingly concentrated on the three sites north of Dorney – Lot's Hole, Lake End Road West and Lake End Road East. The following discussion is focused on these sites, and considers the scarcity or absence of Anglo-Saxon evidence from other sites along the Flood Alleviation Scheme Course. Discussion of the isolated Anglo-Saxon burial found by the Eton Rowing Course Project can be found along with a descriptive summary of the grave and grave goods in Chapter 3.

EARLY SAXON EVIDENCE
by Tim Allen

At the Eton Rowing Course the absence of any significant Saxon or medieval evidence is in marked contrast to the evidence of settlement during the Middle and Late Iron Age and much of the Roman period. The abandonment of the site for permanent settlement appears to have taken place during the later Roman period, as was also the case at Cippenham nearby (Ford 1998). The same is true of Lake End Road West, though there it is argued (Chapter 3) that the boundaries of the Roman occupation survived until the middle Saxon period. A significant shift in settlement location was therefore taking place locally during the later Roman period, though whether this was due to separate but coincidental factors, or a response to wider changes, is unclear.

It is possible that it was the silting up of the palaeochannel of the Thames that flowed through the Rowing Course that put paid to the Roman settlement by its edge, but the failure to relocate settlement within the wider site during the late Roman or Saxon periods must reflect longer-term factors. It is possible that a rise in water table and increased alluviation, as has been claimed in the Upper Thames Valley (Robinson and Lambrick 1984), made the site less habitable. Certainly the present settlements of Dorney and Boveney, first documented, in the late Saxon period, occupy higher and drier areas. This reasoning does not, however, explain the abandonment of settlement at Cippenham, nor at Lake End Road West, and it may have been the wider dislocation of the settlement heirarchy and exchange networks at the end of the Roman period that was responsible.

Elsewhere along the Flood Alleviation Scheme no other evidence of Saxon activity was found. The cereal cultivation evident at Lake End Road West,

and the lone burial near to Boveney, suggest that an Early Saxon settlement existed within the locality, but as yet this remains unlocated.

MIDDLE SAXON EVIDENCE
by Jonathan Hiller and David Petts

The three Dorney excavations produced a body of archaeological evidence striking in character – by virtue of what was not found as much as by what was found. Examination of the various aspects of that evidence leads – as much by elimination as implication – to some unusual conclusions. Overall the evidence suggests that what has been revealed over the three main excavations north of Dorney may best be described as the site of a temporary meeting place, and the following discussion will examine the varied aspects of the evidence to see how they support (or contradict) this hypothesis.

The features

The most striking aspect is that almost all of the features assigned a middle Saxon date, through artefactual dating, stratigraphic relationships, or spatial relationships, were pits. All linear features and structural postholes on the three sites were stratigraphically or artefactually either Roman, related to the Romano-British farmstead (reported in Volume 2) or medieval/post-medieval (this volume). A few dispersed postholes were recorded at Lake End Road West, close to the south edge of the excavation, only one of which (41098), produced middle Saxon dating evidence. The others are undated, and may not be contemporary.

The environment of the region

Direct evidence of vegetation cover from middle Saxon Lot's Hole and Lake End Road in the form of pollen, plant macros and insects was not available. Pollen from a Roman well at Lake End Road West suggests open grassland, with some tree cover, and there is no evidence of a significant change by the middle Saxon period. There are also indications of a hay meadow and implications of a nearby woodland. This is consistent with the indications from the animal bone assemblage, suggesting nearby grazing of livestock. The results from the Eton Rowing Course suggest that some post-Roman alluviation may have occurred, although on the (slightly higher) ground where the Saxon pits were found this probably only meant that the ground surface over the palaeochannels became soft and waterlogged on occasion.

The extent of the activity *(Fig. 5.1)*

A total of 123 features have been assigned a Saxon date on the basis of the finds evidence. These comprise 90 at Lake End Road West, the majority of which were pits of varying sizes, profiles and depths. Twenty features of Saxon date were recorded at Lot's Hole: included in the group were pits and also irregular features (possibly tree-throw holes) from which Saxon pottery was recovered (these are not included in Fig. 3.2). A total of 13 pits were found at Lake End Road East, supplemented by a further three during the watching brief on the adjacent area (although the date of these three features was not established beyond doubt).

Figure 5.1 shows the extent of the pits over the three main sites and the associated watching brief areas. They cover the eastern half of Lake End Road West and the southern parts of Lake End Road East and Lot's Hole. The overall extent of the pits is in the region of 800 m W-E by 300 m N-S, yet it is clear that the limits of the middle Saxon activity have not been reached by the excavations. While the empty areas in northern parts of both Lot's Hole and Lake End Road East suggest a possible northern limit to the activity the spread of pits to the south of Lake End Road West is entirely possible. Within the overall extent of pits as shown in the excavation areas, the principal natural factor governing their distribution seems to be the palaeochannels and adjacent areas which may also have suffered similar seasonal waterlogging; these features are visible on air photographs (see Pl. 1.1). In other words, pits were not dug in areas where the subsoil was prone to any level of waterlogging – the dryness and firmness of the ground was clearly critical. The exception to this is the discrete group of middle Saxon pits at the west end of Lake End Road West; these are considered separately below. There is a clear absence of pits in the east part of the Gravel Storage Area, which does not appear to be due to the presence of a palaeo-channel (see below).

Consideration was given to the possibility of pit alignments, particularly among the large group on the Lake End Road West site (see Fig. 3.1). Pit boundary definitions may be found in urban contexts: excavations at *Hamwic* have demonstrated that pit alignments were used to define property boundaries (Andrews 1997, 179–83). It is apparent that the distribution of pits across the site does respect at least two – and possibly four – broad NW-SE oriented 'paths', and one appears to conform to a defined trackway associated with the Romano-British farmstead. Aside from these 'paths' the arrangement of the pits seems to conform to no linear pattern, and yet their distance from each other is noticeably consistent, and is emphasised by the contrast provided by the discrete group of pits in the far western corner of the site. Here the close, intercutting group of pits suggests a fixed single focus of nearby activity, whereas the infrequency of intercutting pits over the main pit spread is striking. Their distribution is not random, nor is it arranged on a formal landscape or property boundary plan, but it suggests a rationale relating to immediate circumstances.

Chronology *(Fig. 5.2)*

The absence of occupation layers and significant stratigraphic sequences makes it impossible to establish a phased sequence for the middle Saxon features. With very few intercutting pits, there is no stratigraphic reason why the great majority of the pits could not have been open simultaneously, and the entire sequence of pits could have been dug over a very short period of time, perhaps as little as a year. Chronological dating is based almost entirely on artefacts, augmented in some instances by radio-carbon dates (see Chapter 4, Radiocarbon dating).

Analysis of the Saxon finds assemblage indicates that the bulk of the activity at Lake End Road and Lot's Hole can be broadly assigned to the period from the 7th to the 9th centuries. Some features contained decorated pottery that, taken in isolation, could be typologically dated to the 6th century or even earlier; decorated sherds recovered from pits at Lot's Hole and Lake End Road East are of types thought to have gone out of circulation by the end of the 6th century (see Chapter 4, Anglo-Saxon pottery). No decorated sherds were recovered from Lake End Road West. In general the local chaff tempered pottery types may be dated to both the early and late Saxon period.

The general date suggested by the local pottery can be refined by the presence of imported wares, specifically 3 sherds of Ipswich Ware pottery, 18 sherds North French ware, and 3 sherds of Tating Ware at Lake End Road West. Ipswich Ware is generally thought to have been in circulation between *c* AD 650–850, with traded vessel sherds being recovered from archaeological contexts dated after *c* 725, and is interpreted by Blinkhorn to inform on the date of the 'locally made' grass-tempered pottery wares found in the pits. In terms of the pottery, the Saxon activity here is broadly contemporary with the middle Saxon site at Old Windsor, which has been interpreted as a small farmstead or village in the late 7th and early 8th centuries (Wilson and Hurst 1958) and where 8th century Tating Ware and Ipswich ware was recovered. This type of artefactual evidence points to influence of trade and exchange in the middle Saxon period, and it is likely that traders were making contacts at both Old Windsor and Dorney via the River Thames.

Radiocarbon dating of five animal bone samples (one from Lot's Hole, four from Lake End Road West) gives a date range of between the middle of the 7th century and the 9th/10th century (see Chapter 4, Radiocarbon dating). In contrast, radio-carbon dating was also undertaken on charred grain

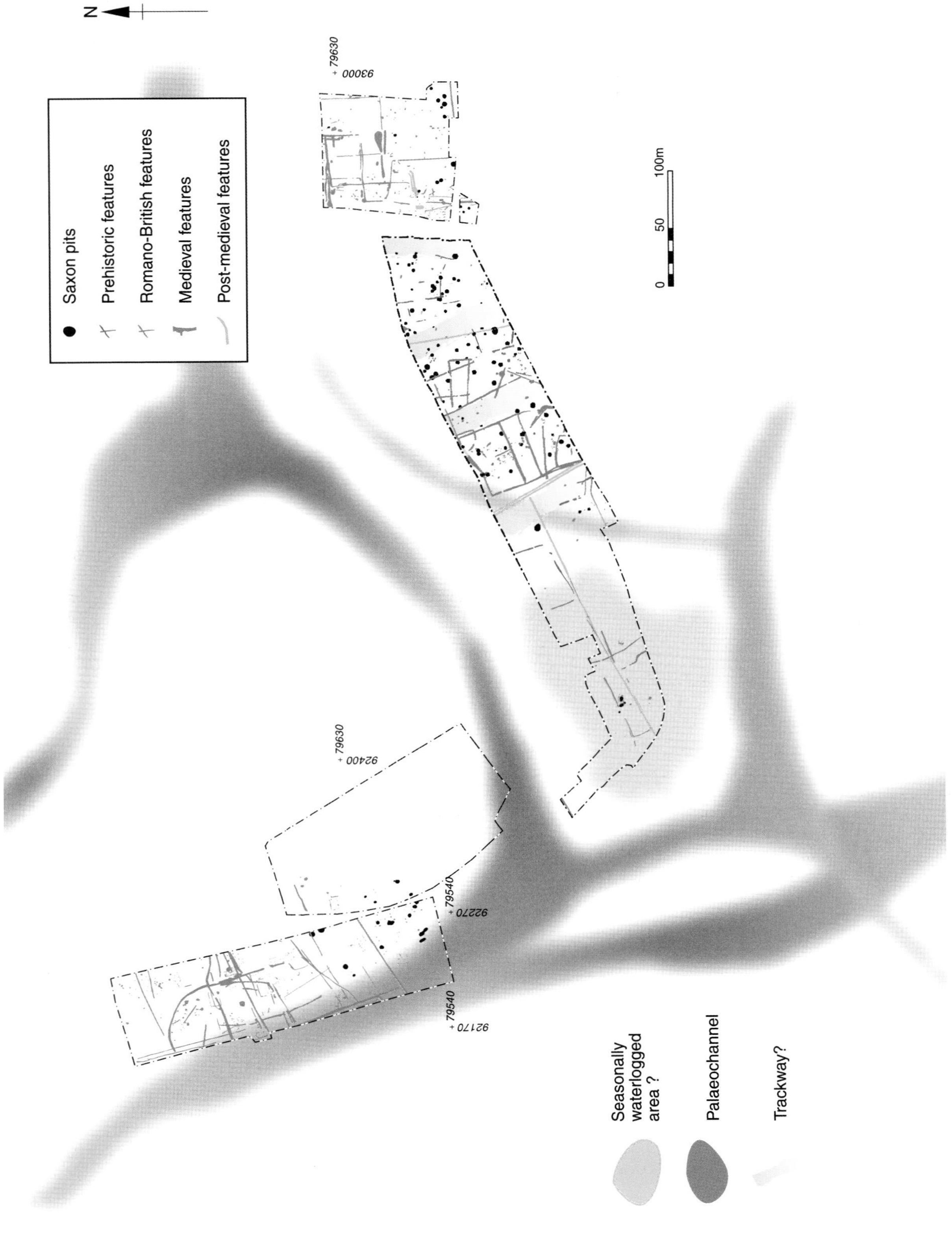

Figure 5.1 *All Anglo-Saxon pits and palaeochannels*

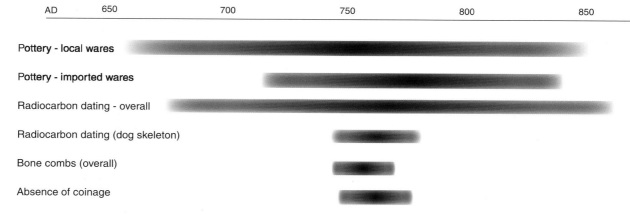

Figure 5.2 Pit chronology: comparative dating estimates

from one of the Saxon pits (40697), which gave a date range between the mid 5th and mid 7th centuries, given the relative confidence rating of the calibrated values. However, these earlier dates came from a feature which also contained a pottery assemblage reliably dated to the later 8th century by the presence of Ipswich ware and imported continental wares. It follows that the grain may have been residual, possibly derived from small scale agricultural activity on the site prior to the main period of use. If the grain can be residual, so could the (possibly) early pottery.

The bone combs provide further evidence for a middle Saxon date. Riddler (Chapter 4, Bone and antler objects) notes that several of the combs can be directly paralleled with combs found in middle Saxon contexts at Hamwic, Ipswich and London, though it should be noted that some of these could be assigned a later date on typological grounds. One comb in particular may date as late as the 10th century. Of the other worked bone artefacts, the pig fibula pin has been assigned a middle-late Saxon date on the basis of comparison with items from Ipswich and York, while the pin beaters can also be directly paralleled with artefacts from middle Saxon Ipswich and Canterbury.

The fragments of glass do not appear to be out of place in Saxon contexts of 6th-8th century date, and many of the iron knives have parallels at middle Saxon York, while the remainder are characteristic of Saxon knives generally. The clay loomweights appear also to fit the generally accepted trend of loomweight development in the Saxon period, and can be placed in the middle Saxon period accordingly.

Although the majority of the material from the sites fits within the broad middle Saxon dating of *c* 700–900, it could fit quite happily in the narrower band of the period from *c* 740 to *c* 780, with a few possible typological exceptions. Figure 5.2 illustrates the varied date spans determined by absolute and typological dating. Within the context of the plausible stratigraphic timespan involved, it would be consistent with the activity happening over as short

a period as a single year within that span – around the year 760.

The character of the archaeology

Over the three excavation sites and the associated watching briefs, a number of buildings were identified, represented by rectilinear alignments of postholes and beam slots. With two exceptions these are securely datable to post 10th-century phases of occupation. The exceptions are two buildings in the central part of Lake End Road West. One has produced secure 2nd-century dating; the other is not artefactually dated. It cuts 1st-century features, and appears to be aligned on later Romano-British ditches, and for these reasons it is tentatively assigned to the later Roman period. There is no evidence to link it in any way to the middle Saxon activity.

The apparent absence of any significant middle Saxon features apart from pits should obviously not be accepted without question. Over such a large area one would typically expect to see evidence of buildings in the form of beam slots or postholes, or paddocks or ditches denoting plot or field divisions. Pits have been found associated with rural settlements such as at Mucking, Essex (Hamerow 1993) and Maxey, Northants (Addyman 1964), while at urban centres such as *Hamwic* buildings and pits are also often found in close proximity (Andrews 1997). Even the depressions of sunken featured buildings, although more common in the 7th century and earlier, would not be totally out of place in a 8th century context. Could it be that all structural evidence has been completely truncated by later activity?

The possibility was considered that ploughing had removed the archaeological evidence for Saxon buildings at Lake End Road West (OAU 1998); in theory buildings of shallow sill beam or posthole construction (ibid.) could have been entirely truncated by later activity. However, over all three sites, and particularly at Lake End Road West where the largest pit group is, the survival of other structures of earlier (Bronze Age, Roman) and later (medieval) periods strongly suggests that total destruction of structural remains by truncation could not have taken place.

Support for the contention that there were no buildings interspersed among the pits is provided by some aspects of finds assemblage, in particular the absence of significant quantities of daub or structural remains such as iron door hinges or roves. Only a small proportion of the clay recovered from the pit fills exhibited wattle impressions that is typical of daub used as wall covering, and that could as likely have come from ovens.

The western pit group

In sharp contrast to the extensive and dispersed spread of pits extending over the three sites, a small, very localised group of intercutting pits – of broadly similar date but generally shallower – were identified at the west end of Lake End Road West. It is suggested that they represent a focus of activity that is unrelated to the activity represented by the main group of pits. It is notable that unlike all the others, these pits are situated in an area that, from the evidence of the air photos, was surrounded by palaeochannels and may well have been significantly more affected by waterlogging. The ground conditions here may also have a bearing on the absence of structural remains in the vicinity of the pits. The softer subsoil would arguably have led to progressively deeper disturbance caused by ploughing in later periods, which could have truncated structural evidence that would have survived on the gravel islands to the north-east and east. To support this hypothesis, it is significant that, after a consistent depth of topsoil was machine-stripped from all three sites, the only vestiges of medieval ridge-and-furrow that survived underneath were located in the south-western corner of Lot's Hole, where a palaeochannel runs, and the western third of Lake End Road West, in the area of possible waterlogging.

The pits and their fills

Broadly speaking there are four pit types represented on the three main excavations (see Fig. 3.4):

Type 1 – Large irregular shaped, cut deep into the gravel

Type 2 – Circular, steep-sided, cut deep into the gravel

Type 3 – Circular, steep-sided, extended 'funnel' base cut into the gravel

Type 4 – Shallow profiled, often irregular shape or circular

The majority of the pits do not appear to have been dug initially for the sole purpose of rubbish disposal, as there are few, if any finds from the majority of the primary fills. The Type 1 pits are very large, and are interpreted as water holes, possibly to service livestock. Pit 40260 at Lake End Road West has one relatively shallow sloping side, possibly to allow access into the feature. The fact that this pit is located some distance west of the main pit group may suggest that it was dug here to provide water for livestock, perhaps cattle or horses, that were kept away from the main focus of activity.

The Type 2 and 3 pits were steep sided and dug to a considerable depth, with some exhibiting funnel-shaped profiles towards the base. The lack of any evidence of linings to these pits would not be significant if they were intended as only temporary sources of water. The Type 4 pits could arguably be too shallow even for temporary water holes; a possible alternative may be that they were small quarries to produce gravel for localised temporary surfaces or pathways.

The pit fill sequences

The filling sequences of all of the pits at Lake End Road and Lot's Hole share very similar characteristics. Typically, the primary fills consisted of clean, interleaved layers of silt and gravel, resulting from the natural erosion of the pit sides, or gravel material and water-borne silts. Some of the primary fills had a humic element characteristic of cess that may indicate that some of the pits were initially used as latrines, or receptacles for cess (see also Macphail's report on the soil micromorphology on the CD-ROM, who has noted phosphates within the pits analysed). Pits dug specifically for the receipt of cess are noted at *Hamwic* (Andrews 1997). Finds from the primary pit deposits were limited to single sherds of pottery and some animal bone; they were therefore not primary rubbish disposal features.

The secondary or middle fills appear to be the result of episodes of rubbish disposal. These fills exhibited well-defined tip lines, in some cases alternating clean gravel layers with layers of charcoal- and bone-rich refuse, the result perhaps of fires and episodes of cooking (?feasting). The secondary fills usually contained rich assemblages of animal bones, artefacts and charred plant remains.

Macphail's analysis suggests that the secondary pit fills were thoroughly sorted by mesofauna indicating that the biological activity kept pace with the rate of infill. This implies that the rate of infill was gradual in the middle stages. Groundwater appears also to have affected the pit fills, again indicative of intermittent infilling of individual pits.

The final pit fills were typically dark and thick, homogeneous deposits with few tip lines. Artefacts and animal bones were generally relatively abundant, as was redeposited Roman tile and pottery and flints. The condition of the finds recovered from the upper fills differed little from the quality of preservation of the finds from the middle fills; in general finds preservation was good throughout the pit fill sequences.

The mechanism of refuse deposition in the pits (Fig. 5.3)

Closer examination of the pit fills and the finds within them can shed light on the nature of the activity over the area. An analysis of the pit fills needs to consider the varying processes through which the objects entered them. There has been little study of Anglo-Saxon patterns of refuse deposition (along the lines of Hill (1995) for the Iron Age) so there is little comparative work against which to compare these pits. It is possible, however, to construct three models of refuse deposition against which to test the data, derived primarily from the Lake End Road West pits.

The main variable in these models is the extent to which the rubbish enters the features directly from the use areas; does it enter the pit directly or is it mediated through secondary processes, such as middening?

Model 1

In this model the refuse in the pits is derived from a central midden through which all refuse on the site passes. The consequences of such a system would be that all the refuse in the pits will have gone through the same post-depositional processes and that the composition of the pit assemblages should be fairly homogeneous, as they will all be drawn from the same source.

Model 2

In this model each separate area of activity has its own midden through which rubbish passes before entering the pits. This pattern of refuse disposal would lead to different pit assemblages from those in Model 1; the pit contents would be more hetero-geneous, reflecting the different origins of the rubbish. In addition, whilst lying in open middens refuse may be more open to post-depositional processes than refuse protected within pits; for example bone in middens may be more susceptible to chewing and gnawing by dogs and rodents than bone in a pit. If the middens were primarily formed to create manure then the presence of manuring scatters of pottery and other debris located by fieldwalking, would also provide some circumstantial evidence for the existence of middens on or near the site.

Model 3

In this third model the refuse enters the pit directly. In terms of assemblage composition it may be difficult to distinguish between Models 2 and 3, though the process of middening in Model 2 may lead to a greater level of fragmentation. However, it should be possible to distinguish between the two models on the basis of pit formation. Deposits derived from Model 2 processes would be composed of large dumps of material, as the middens were transferred to the pits in one or two discrete events. Pit contents created through Model 3 processes are instead formed through an ongoing series of dumps over a period of time.

The pit contents

The contents of the pits appear to be superficially similar, containing pot, bone and a range of small finds including combs, querns, loomweights and knives, as well as a large quantity of slag and other ironworking by-products. However, a closer examination of the pit contents shows that there is a wide variation in the pit fills. If the quantity of bone and pot within the pits is compared it is clear that there is no relationship between the two; a pit containing a large amount of pot does not necessarily contain a large number of bones.

The heterogeneity is also seen in the variation in the size of pottery assemblage. Although assemblages of Fabric 1 and Fabric 2 ceramic fragments cluster around 0–10 level in each pit, there are several much larger assemblages. However the level of fragmentation found in these larger assemblages (as indicated by the ratio of sherd number to assemblage weight) is broadly the same as for the smaller groups of pot. This implies that despite the variation in assemblage size the pot appears to have gone through the same post-depositional processes.

A further indicator of the heterogeneity of the pit assemblages can be seen in the relative proportions of Fabrics 1 and 2 in the pottery assemblages. If the deposits were derived from a mixed central midden one would expect to find fairly consistent proportions of the two fabrics in the pits. However this is not borne out by the evidence. Around one third of all pits contained no Fabric 1, and an equal amount contain no Fabric 2, with the rest containing mixed assemblages.

The animal bone material is more complex – no attempt has been made to explore comparative fragmentation of bone assemblages due to the large number of variables that affect the fragility of animal bone. However, there is a wide variation in the proportions of the bones from the main domesticates from the Lake End Road West pits, as well as in the body parts represented (see Chapter, Animal bone and CD-ROM). Animal bones were clearly subject to a series of post-depositional processes before entering the pits.

The evidence from the pottery and bone suggests a wide level of heterogeneity in the composition of the pit assemblages, with little evidence that the fills were derived from the same source. This leads us to reject Model 1 (central midden). However, such wide variety in pit fills would satisfy the conditions for both Models 2 and 3. One way of distinguishing between material which had been deposited straight into a pit and material which had been left in a midden for a period before entering the pits is to explore further the evidence for the taphonomic

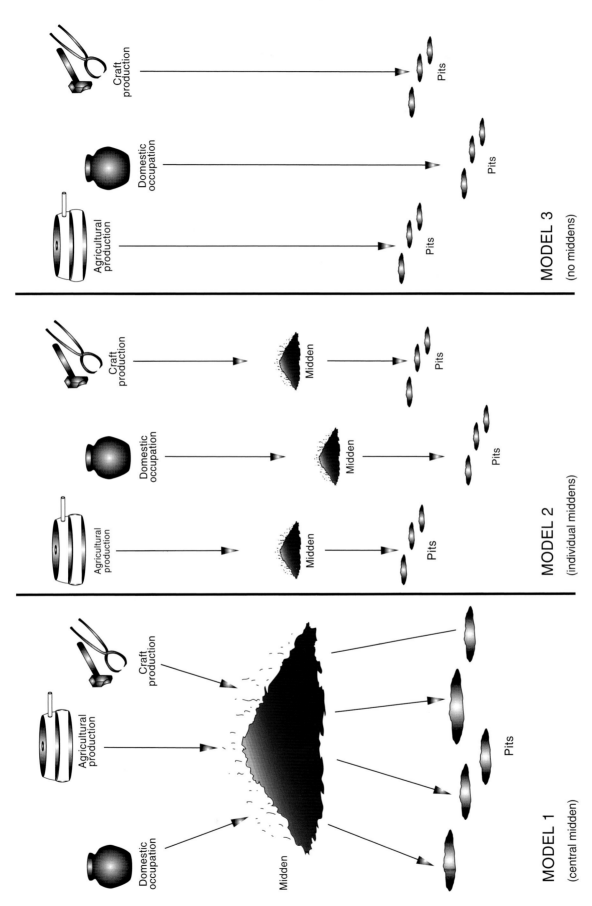

Figure 5.3 *Refuse deposition models*

processes exerted on the material. One immediately noticeable factor is the relatively high level of gnawing on the animal bones (18% of the material); this compares to only 4% of the bone from the mid-Saxon excavations at *Hamwic* (Bourdillon with Andrews 1997, 243). This suggests that at *Hamwic* the animal bone entered the pits quickly, before dogs had an opportunity to chew it, whereas at Lake End Road West the bone appears to have been accessible to dogs for a period of time before entering the pits.

The pattern of fill sequences displays some ambiguities; the middle layers suggest a series of relatively small tips over a period of time, with occasional lenses of clean gravel, which would be consistent with Model 3 refuse disposal, whilst the upper layers tend to be thick, dark, more homogeneous deposits with few tip lines, which could suggest rapid infilling or the dumping of midden deposits (Model 2). This might imply that there were two different strategies for rubbish disposal on the site; continuous events of rubbish disposal in the pits, as well as the creation of middens, which were dumped into the top of pits towards the end of the pits life. Reasons for these two alternate strategies are not clear. It is unclear whether the deposition of the midden deposits in the upper layers was a planned exercise in order to fill up the pits and level-up the land surface at one point in time, or whether it was an on-going process of sealing the pits as they began to fill up. Alternatively the middle layers may primarily have been small-scale refuse disposal on an individual or small group level, possibly to seal cess deposits; the midden deposits may represent more organised acts of disposal, possibly at a house-

hold level or higher level. Whether such organised midden-clearing took place periodically during the duration of the 'occupation' of the site, or after the site was deserted is unclear.

No clear indication of 'placed' deposits was found. The presence of a complete dog skeleton (42089, Pl. 5.1) in a middle fill of pit 41234 is most likely to represent the simple disposal of a dog which had died – possibly from injuries, judging by the evidence of previous traumas on the bones (see CD ROM Clark in Saxon animal bone).

The possibility that the upper fills of the pits could be the result of later ploughing dragging artefactually rich topsoil into the part-filled pits cannot be ruled out, although two aspects argue against this. Firstly, the condition of the finds in the upper pit fills was not appreciably worse than the material from the lower fills, which might be expected if the material had been abraded and worn by plough disturbance; secondly, one might expect a richer assemblage of finds to have remained in the topsoil to be recovered by fieldwalking, and this was not the case.

Residuality and reuse

An important element of the finds assemblage from Anglo-Saxon pits was Roman finds, suggesting either a level of residuality or active reuse of Roman material culture. The occurrence level of Roman objects in Anglo-Saxon pits varied according to artefact type. For example 10% (by weight) of Romano-British tile was unstratified, 67% in post-Roman contexts and only 23% was found within

Plate 5.1   Lake End Road West: dog skeleton in pit 41234

Romano-British features. This contrasts with the Roman pottery where 50% was from unstratified contexts, 47% from secure Romano-British contexts and only 3.3% from Anglo-Saxon contexts. Clearly different Roman objects were subject to different post-depositional processes.

It is unlikely that the tile in Anglo-Saxon deposits was derived from on-site Roman features, as there is a lack of Roman structures on site of a type that might be expected to have a tiled roof. This implies that most Roman tile, both in Roman and Anglo-Saxon features must be from an external source. The tile could have arrived from this source in one of two ways, either as deliberately curated or reused material, or alternatively as a residual component of refuse deposits derived from an area with higher levels of Roman material culture. The lack of residual Roman pottery associated with the Roman tile implies that the former of the two alternatives is more likely.

The reason for the curation of the tile is unclear. There is no burning or scorching to indicate their use as hearth bases, neither has the Anglo-Saxon material produced evidence for any industrial activity that might reuse Roman tile. However, they may have had a range of uses, such as pot stands, which do not leave archaeological traces.

The finds

Aspects of the finds assemblage support the hypothesis of a temporary meeting place – some of these have been suggested already in the context of the absence of permanent buildings.

Activities on the site

Alongside these suggestions of status and affluence are some – but importantly not many – indicators of craft or light industrial activity. Slight patterns of disposal of some categories of artefact are evident (see Figs 5.4–5), hinting at some form of loose organisation of activities on site.

The most prominent of these is represented by the substantial deposits of slag from the site, and these seem to be particularly concentrated in a confined part of Lake End Road West (see Fig. 5.5). The assemblage weighed over 46 kg, the bulk of which represented secondary smithing. The majority of the slag took the form of smithing hearth bottoms, which form due to the accumulation of iron silicate material produced during smithing, collecting at the base of a hearth. No evidence for iron smelting was forthcoming to suggest that here was a primary manufacturing site, and the limited presence of hammerscale suggests that the hearth bottoms were discarded into the open pits as soon as the hearth became unworkable. Only a small proportion of vitrified hearth lining material was recovered (28 g).

The Lake End Road ironworking compares poorly with that from Ramsbury, Wiltshire. It is clear that the Ramsbury site represents a specific iron smelting works using imported iron ore. Haslam has postulated that the site was part of a *villa regalis*, based on the fact that the site was in close proximity to the site of a Roman *vicus*, and it is suggested that Ramsbury was the centre of one of a number of important estates in that region, based on the Kennet Valley (Haslam 1980). The site at Lake End Road does not fall into this category, we lack for instance the hearths and fire pits that characterise the site at Ramsbury. Lake End Road West appears to be a secondary production site, as stated above, perhaps working articles on the site. A temporary smith may be expected for instance to work horse equipment, blades and other agricultural tools, for the use of the local populace, though little of this evidence was recovered from the excavations.

A small fragment of copper alloy casting waste may indicate the production or repair of copper alloy objects, but this was clearly on a very small scale. Four small fragments of lead strip and offcuts were found in Anglo-Saxon contexts, all from Lot's Hole, although the vast majority of such items and all the melted lead waste were found in the spoil. The presence of an iron chisel or punch and a possible awl from Lake End Road West is indicative of carpentry but they are general purpose tools, not indicative of any particular specialist activity.

The animal bone assemblage is large, but contains no evidence for specialist craft activities, such as bone working or tanning.

Textile equipment (Pl. 4.6)

A range of textile equipment was recovered from site, producing evidence for all stages of cloth production. The evidence for the presence – if not necessarily the production – of raw materials was evident in the presence of flax capsules and the presence of plentiful quantities of sheep bones from the site. However, the age profile of the sheep suggests they were being slaughtered primarily for meat rather than wool, and the flax capsules may also have been used for the production of linseed oil and for animal fodder.

Primary processing of the wool can be seen in the presence of a number of wool-comb teeth and a substantial part of a wool-comb (Fig. 4.5 no. 4 SF 42835, context 41733, pit 41700) used for combing the wool prior to spinning. The wool-comb has an iron binding indicating it is unlikely to be a flax heckle (Walton Rogers 1997, 1731). The other so-called heckle teeth are between 65 and 95 mm long; Walton Rogers suggests that, in York at least, teeth from flax heckles are 60–85 mm long and those from wool combs 90–110 mm long (ibid.) This might be taken to indicate the presence of both types of tool on site, but the fragmentary nature of teeth found on the sites means it is difficult to be certain of their original length; it would be difficult to argue for definite evidence of flax processing (there is also a noticeable

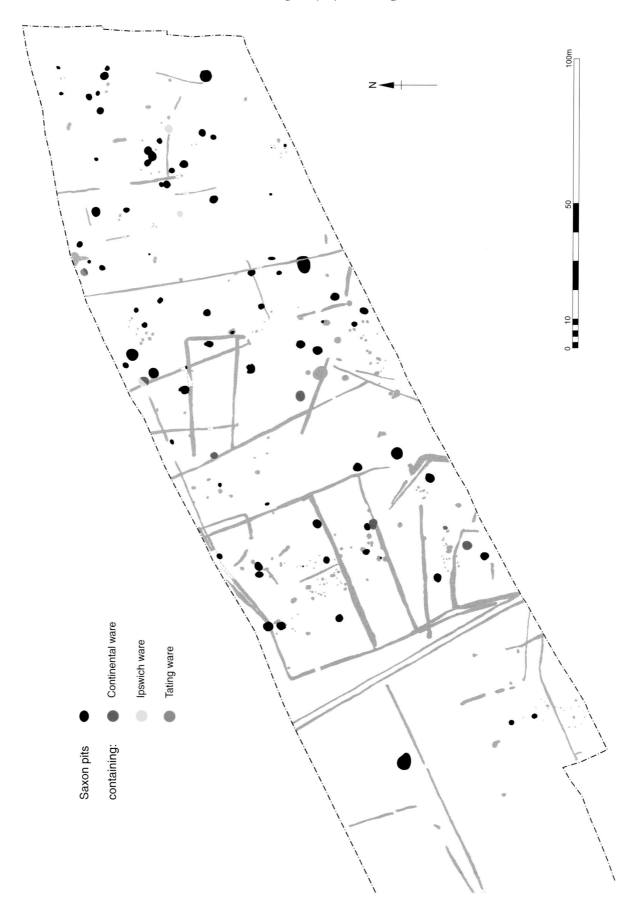

Saxon pits

containing:

Continental ware

Ipswich ware

Tating ware

Figure 5.4   Lake End Road West: distribution plot of imported pottery

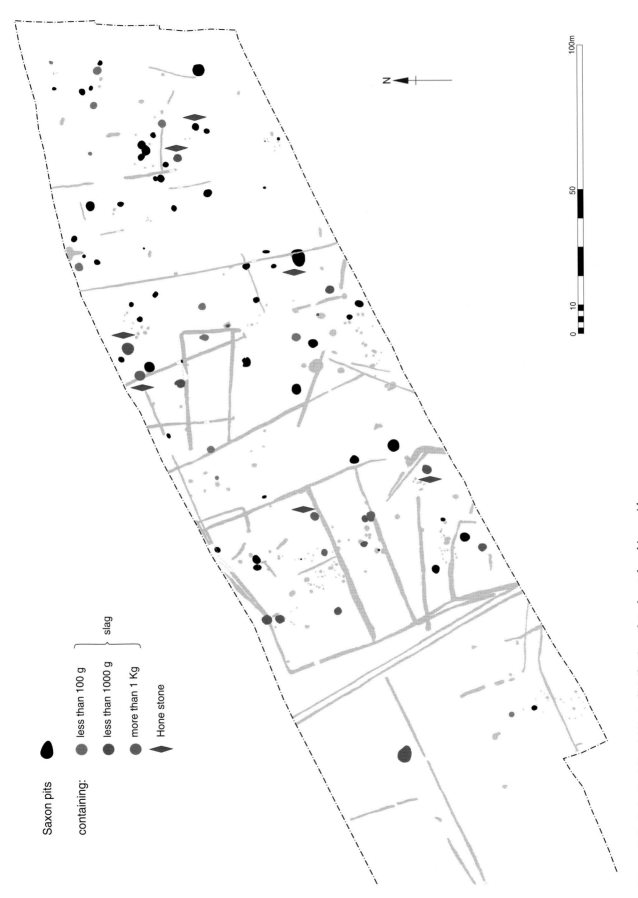

Figure 5.5 Lake End Road West: distribution plot of metalworking evidence

lack of linen smoothers from the site). The blades from a set of shears (SF 42799, context 41671, pit 41593) may have been used for shearing or the cutting of cloth.

The assemblage is notable for its paucity of spindlewhorls. Only two are known from the three sites: half a burnt, plano-convex Greensand whorl (Fig. 4.7.3 SF 42795, context 40405, pit 40356) and a fired-clay example (SF 45103, context 41992). A fragmentary, but highly polished bone object may be a lathe-turned bone spindle, though possibly of Roman date (context 41542, pit 41541). It is tempting to suggest that this supports the contention that no spinning was occurring on this transient site, and that still may be the case, although only two spindlewhorls (and a single loomweight) were recovered from the middle Saxon 'permanent' site at Maxey (Addyman 1964, 58).

More evidence is forthcoming for weaving with the assemblage of fired clay loomweights (see Chapter 4, Fired clay objects). It was only possible to identify 29 of the 237 loomweights by type: 22 are intermediate and 7 were bun-shaped (according to Hurst's classification; Hurst 1959). Decoration appeared on both types. One intermediate loomweight had a ring stamp on the clay ring, whilst a bun-shaped weight was decorated with rows of stabbed dots and a possible ring stamp. These paralleled decorations found on similar weights from Old Erringham (Holden 1976, fig. 3.1–2), and Ramsbury (Haslam 1980, fig. 19.3). The presence of such loomweights suggests that at least one warp-weighted loom was being used on site. The lack of single large groups of weights and the secondary nature of the pit deposits from which most of the weights were recovered makes it difficult to establish the number of looms being used on site, yet it seems reasonable to conclude that it must have been a fairly small-scale activity. As a measure one may note the 180 plus loomweights from Mucking (Hamerow 1993, 66) and the 200 plus from West Stow (West 1985, 138).

Other evidence for weaving is found with the assemblage of eight double-pointed bone pin-beaters, which were used for beating down individual threads in the weft of the cloth. Six were definitely made of antler and the remaining two probably were. They were circular and oval in cross-section and varied in length from 104–92 mm. In size they were broadly comparable to examples from Brandon, Canterbury, *Hamwic*, Ipswich, London, North Elmham, and Shakenoak (Blockley *et al.* 1995, 1173; Cowie *et al.* 1988, 137, fig. 38.8; Wade-Martins 1980, fig. 260.18, 22–3; Brodribb *et al.* 1972, fig. 62.3) corresponding best with those from rural sites (eg Brandon and Shakenoak) rather than those from urban contexts. However, the longest pin-beater (context 40326, pit 40487, SF 40292) is best paralleled from middle Saxon urban sites such as Canterbury, *Hamwic*, Ipswich and York, and long and short pin-beaters may have had complementary functions.

Food provision

The animal bone assemblage has characteristics in common with high status consumer sites, rather than producer sites. Most of the pig, sheep and cattle were arriving at the site on the hoof, at their prime ages for culling for meat. All of the stages of carcass processing were in evidence on site, but no large deposits of bone were found in individual pits. The specific butchery pit seen on other middle Saxon consumer sites – for instance pit 394 at the middle Saxon minster at Eynsham (Hardy *et al.* forthcoming) – was not in evidence here. In other words the butchery seems to have been undertaken on an unsystematic and ad hoc basis.

From the charred plant remains, a wide range of cereals – barley, wheat, oats, and rye were being processed on the site. The presence of emmer wheat in one sample is intriguing – and it was radiocarbon dated to the period cal AD 430–660 (NZA-9206; 1487 ± 58BP). Its presence within a deposit also containing reliably dated 8th century middle Saxon pottery (Ipswich ware and Continental wares) suggests the emmer wheat must be residual, presumably a relic from earlier activity on the site. Pelling suggests that the evidence of all the primary stages of crop processing implies a degree of permanence – the site would have to be occupied to some degree through the spring, summer and autumn. However, this argument assumes that the crops were being cultivated at or very near to the site, for which there is no supporting archaeological evidence.

Another artefact that may indicate food provision – if perhaps on a more opportunistic basis – is an antler bow-guard from Lot's Hole (SF 50214). It was decorated on one side with repeated curvilinear designs within a frame formed by a single bounding line. The pattern consists of two curved and two oblique lines with pecked decoration applied across the available space; the design may represent stylised birds. This may suggest the target of any archery on site – the hunting of wildfowl – which is also attested by the bone assemblage.

There are also hints that fishing may have occurred near the site. One of the bone needles from site may have been a netting needle (context 41615, pit 41616), and the lead weight and rolled scraps of lead sheeting may have been used as net weights (cf. Mainman and Rogers 2000, 2534–5). However, there is relatively little evidence from the bone assemblage that fish played a significant part in the diet at these sites, although the evidence points to some of the fish coming from the Thames estuary, which is slight evidence for river trade.

Food processing

The artefactual evidence for food production is limited to the presence of quernstones, indicating some level of cereal processing on the site. Most of the quernstones were manufactured from Niedermendig lava from the Rhineland, although one small millstone was made from feldspathic sandstone, which may be a German Triassic sandstone, possibly from the Eiffel district. Similar stone was used for artefacts found at Dorestad (Kars 1983, 27). More local Surrey Greensand was also used for a few querns.

Roe (see CD-ROM Worked Stone section) notes the generally small size of the lava quern fragment assemblage and suggests that it may indicate that some quern 'roughouts' were being completed on this site. However, it should be noted that no fragment of quern 'roughout' itself was recovered from the excavations. The few recognisable quern fragments that were found had clearly been well used, in some instances worn down to a thickness of only *c* 25 mm from a probable original thickness of *c* 60 mm (based on parallels from Dorestad, Kars 1980, 412).

Who was here and why?

Turning to what the finds say about the type and status of people gathered here, and why they were gathered, the finds analyses have raised interesting contradictions.

The personal possessions among the finds assemblage suggest an affluence or status that would not be out of place in an urban or *wic* situation, but is untypical in what appears to be a remote rural setting. For instance, a number of finds – the bone combs – both in quality and number (Fig. 4.8 & Pl. 4.4), the imported pottery (Pl. 4.1), the inlaid bucket handle (Pl. 4.3), or the vessel glass all attest to the presence of people with disposable wealth. Another indicator of the presence of private and possibly valuable possessions on the site is the fragmentary remains of a number of locks and padlocks. Two keys, a possible padlock case and possible parts of barb-spring padlock bolt all attest to an interest in securing possessions, though the presence of padlocks rather than door-locks and the lack of any structural ironwork such as roves or hinges known from other middle Anglo-Saxon settlements (eg Fishergate, Rogers 1993, 1409–13) suggests they may have been used to secure boxes or chests rather than doors.

These aspects might also be seen as an indicator of trade, and such a possibility could be supported by the presence of the imported material, like the querns (see above) or the pottery (see Chapter 4, Anglo-Saxon pottery and Chronology above). It is possible that the exotic pottery types (Ipswich, Tating and Northern French wares) may be indicators of a high status activity on the site, but this assumption needs close consideration.

Ipswich ware is commonly found in East Anglia (Norfolk and Suffolk) where it appears to act as the standard local pottery ware and was probably not used as a marker of status (Blinkhorn 1999, 5). However, outside this core area the distribution of Ipswich ware was considerably more limited. In the peripheral area of Ipswich Ware distribution the pottery can be found at a range of sites from important ecclesiastical sites such as Brixworth and Barking Abbey (Cramp *et al.* 1977; Redknap 1991) to major trading sites such as London (Blackmore 1988) and rural sites, such as Raunds (Blinkhorn forthcoming). Blinkhorn has suggested that the further away from its East Anglian core region Ipswich ware is found, the more likely it is to be an indicator of high status. However there is nothing inherent in the presence of Ipswich ware at Lake End Road which needs to suggest automatically that its presence is an indicator of high status. Its apparent low status within the core area of its distribution may well imply that when it is found outside this area it may well have not been the primary object of trade, but instead accompanied less archaeologically visible commodities. In later 8th century London it was the dominant coarse ware (Blackmore 1997), and given the easy access of Dorney to London via the Thames it is not surprising that the occasional fragment of Ipswich ware arrived on the site. Its presence on site may merely reflect its popularity at its nearest *wic* site.

A similar pattern can be seen with the distribution of foreign imports. They are common at *wic* sites, where they entered the country (eg *c* 12% by sherd count from *Hamwic* and *Lundenwic*), but less common the further away one gets away from the focus of the settlement. It seems that imports at such sites are not high status *per se* but being used to supplement an existing range of ceramic wares. The limited amount of imported wares from Dorney (*c* 3% by sherd count) shows that the imported wares are clearly very much a small element of the pottery assemblage. If, as seems likely, the imported pottery was obtained via London, then it is most likely that the vessels were being brought to the site, not as high status objects, but on the back of other more important or substantial traded objects. The one exception to this is perhaps Tating Ware which is genuinely rare, in Western Europe except at the *emporium* of Dorestad. Even with this, the proximity of the sites to the royal palace at Old Windsor, which also has evidence for Tating Ware may help explain the presence of such an unusual ware.

The plausibility or otherwise, of the purpose of the gathering being for trade clearly needs to address the absence of contemporary coinage from all three excavation sites. Through the 8th century, the amount of coinage in circulation in East Anglia and south-east of England fluctuated significantly, and there does appear to have been a period between *c* 740 and *c* 780 when very little minting occurred, and little coinage was in circulation. This conclusion was initially based upon results from excavations within the known commercial centres like *Hamwic* (Andrews and Metcalf 1997), but has more recently been echoed by the findings from (mainly) East Anglian sites. If the absence of coinage from the Dorney area is to be explained by chronological factors rather than as a factor of site status or function then the period of activity at the site needs to be fitted within the window between *c* 740 and

780, which, on the basis of the other dating evidence, is perfectly possible. However, caution is needed; such a logic assumes that the (?main) function of the site was indeed trade.

Overlapping with the category of open-air market sites is that of local and regional meeting or moot sites. Little archaeological research has taken place on such sites, though recent fieldwalking at Cuckhamsley, West Hendred, the site of an important hundred place with wider regional importance has failed to find significant levels of metalwork or coins (Semple pers. comm.), suggesting that exchange would not necessarily have been the primary function of such meeting places.

Given the peripatetic nature of Anglo-Saxon kingship and governance it is to be expected that a range of temporary meeting places might be found in the archaeological record. The evidence from Anglo-Saxon synods suggests that important church meetings could often take place away from important settlement sites. Whilst some synods may have taken place at monastic sites, the names of some unidentified synods, such as *Clofesho* suggest the place is described in topographic or descriptive terms rather than as named settlement sites. The location of synods at *Croft* (field?) and *Æt Astran* (at the kilns) suggests that synods could take place on sites given over to agricultural production or industrial activity rather than a permanent domestic occupation (Cubitt 1995, 35).

Significantly, other sites without apparent structural remains are beginning to be discovered. An example of such a site may be Barham, East Anglia. This site is located on a ridge overlooking the Gipping Valley, 7 km north-west of Ipswich. Excavation of the 6–7 ha site, has so far failed to locate any structures, but has produced significant quantities of Ipswich ware, along with imported pottery, metalwork and coins, leading to the suggestion that the site may have served as a market or open air meeting place. However, as only a very small percentage of the site has been excavated so far, the apparent absence of buildings is a long way from being confirmed (Hamerow 1998, 198–9).

At a wider level synods were often held at the borders of kingdoms, often on rivers (Cubitt 1995); both factors fulfilled by the Dorney site. Whilst it is unlikely that the activity at Dorney was an unknown synod, there must have been a range of lesser religious, pastoral, legal, military and political meetings that took place in Anglo-Saxon England. Like synod sites these locations may well have been used intermittently over a period of years; activity would be repeated but occasional. The Dorney site may represent just such a site. A range of temporary structures may have been used. Eddius Stephanus makes references in his Life of St Wilfrid to King Æeldfrith's thegn creeping out of the King's tent to inform on plots against Wilfrid (1927 *c*. 47); Bede also makes references to '*Tabernaculo solemus itinere vel in bello uti*' (*Epistolas VII*, Hurst 1983, 265). Bishop Ælfsige of Chester-le-Street also stayed in a tent whilst attending a council of King Edgar (Brown 1969, 24).

The organisation of space on the site would not be incompatible with such a meeting location. There is ample provision of watering holes and open space available for the pitching of tents and temporary structures. There is some evidence for craft activity, but not enough to suggest that commercial activity was the raison d'etre of the gathering. The main evidence for agricultural activity is for the grinding of grain, as would be needed to feed a large group of people (Pl. 5.2).

The political background

The sites north of Dorney sit between two important middle/late Anglo-Saxon centres: the royal *vill* and episcopal centre at Cookham and the royal palace site at Old Windsor (see Fig. 1.1). The Thames was an important boundary throughout the Anglo-Saxon period. In the 6th and 7th century it marked the northern boundary of the *regio* of the *Sunningas*, which extended as far east as Chertsey, where it was noted as sharing a common boundary with an estate granted by Friuthwald, sub-king of Surrey, *c* AD 672–4 (S.11165, Blair 1989). To the west it bordered the adjoining *regio* of the *Readingas* to the east of Reading, possibly along the River Loddon. To the north of the Thames the site was probably within the territory of the political entity known as the *Chilternsaetna*, occupying the area of the Chilterns and as far south as the Thames from eastern Hertfordshire to the Goring Gap (Bailey 1989, 111). Little is known about this shadowy kingdom; it may have remained in native British hands for most of the 6th century. The wealthy early 7th-century barrow burial at Taplow may represent the burial of a client king supplied with high status goods through the overlordship of Kentish or East Saxon kings and occupying a location overlooking the major boundary with Wessex (Stephens 1884). Whilst the lands to the south of the Thames passed to and from Mercian control their grip north of the river appears to have been tighter and the area probably remained under Mercian control until Wessex and Mercia were amalgamated in the early 10th century.

The area immediately south of the Thames was a bone of contention between Mercia and Wessex, particularly in the later 8th century. This can be seen in the history of the monastery at Cookham. It was clearly under Mercian control during the rule of Aethelbald who gave the monastery to the Archbishop of Canterbury (S.1258/B291; Yorke 1995, 62). However, Cynewulf, King of Wessex, took advantage of the crisis in Mercian politics following the murder of Aethelbald to bribe members of the Archbishop's household to steal the title deeds of Cookham and took over the monastery and estate for himself. Nonetheless by AD 798 a record of a dispute concerning the monastery notes that the monastery and 'many other towns of Wessex' had been seized by Offa from Cynewulf of Wessex.

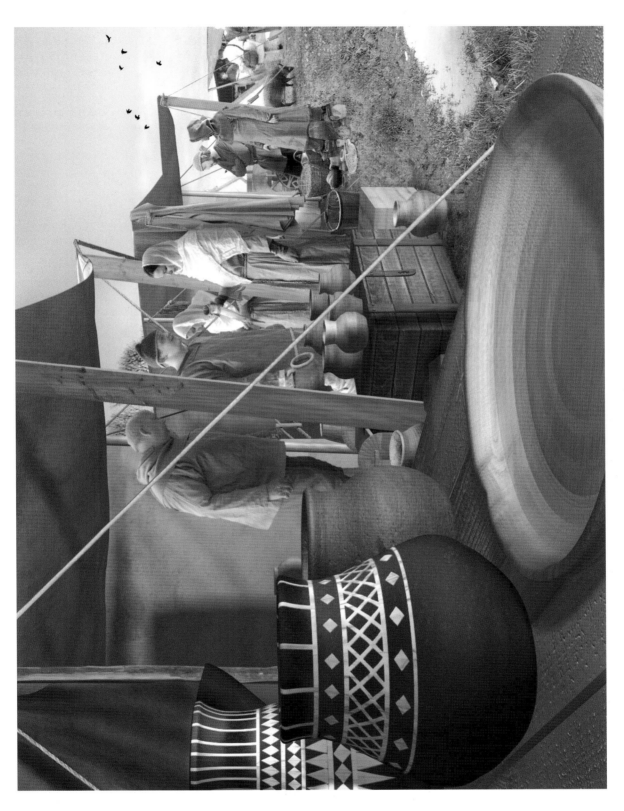

Plate 5.2 Reconstruction of the Anglo-Saxon site during the gathering

This may have followed Offa's defeat of Cynewulf at Bensington in AD 779 (Whitelock 1961, 33). Berkshire (or at least its northern part) remained Mercian territory well into the 9th century, and was recorded as such in a charter of Beorhtwulf in AD 844, only being returned to West Saxon control a few years later.

The strategic importance is reflected by the placement of the Burghal fort of *Sceaftesege*, possibly located on the neighbouring island of Sashes (Brooks 1971). This is one of a series of burhs located on the Thames listed in the Burghal Hidage, including Cricklade, Wallingford, Oxford and Southwark (Hill 1981, fig. 150). Although most burhs were created in response to the Viking threat, Offa had enforced the construction of fortifications in Mercia, and Wessex inherited a system of pre-existing fortifications within Mercia, so *Sceaftesege* has the potential to be an earlier foundation. It certainly fills in a gap in Haslam's map of possible Mercian burhs between London and Oxford (Brooks 1971; Haslam 1987).

Old Windsor, although excavated, remains unpublished. By the 11th century it was clearly a royal palace of Edward the Confessor and was recorded as a *villa regalis* in a charter of 1065. Occupation appears to have begun much earlier though, as a number of sunken featured buildings were identified. Other structures from the site included at least two rectilinear halls and two successive mills (one with a late 7th century dendrochronology date). A 'huge' ditch of 7th-8th century date was also recorded. Little is know about the finds assemblage, though Tating Ware was recovered (Dunning *et al.* 1959).

In a wider regional context the Thames gave the area easy access to London. The city had been captured by Aethelbald and *Lundenwic* became Mercia's most important *emporium*. London was one of the major entry points for trade with the Continent, despite a brief trading dispute between Offa and Charlemagne in AD 790-7.

In conclusion the Dorney sites were located on an important border between Mercia and Wessex, though whilst the lands immediately to the south of the river changed hands several times, South Buckinghamshire probably remained firmly in Mercian hands. In the period from *c* 780 to *c* 850 when most of East Berkshire was under the control of Mercia, the actual southern border of the kingdom probably ran along the Icknield Way (Stenton 1913, 23-5). The two major sites in the region, Cookham and Old Windsor, were both high status, though the royal identity of Old Windsor is only attested in the 11th century. The Dorney site's position on the Thames gave it easy access to both these sites and to the *emporium* of London further downstream.

CONCLUSION

Increasingly a range of new settlement categories are being recognised in the middle Anglo-Saxon archaeological record, moving away from the simple categories of rural site, palace site, monastery and *emporium/wic*. The rapid increase of so-called 'productive sites' mainly stimulated by metal detector finds, has shown that the pre-Viking settlement hierarchy is more subtle and graded than previously perceived (see Ulmschneider 2000; Richards 1999).

Dorney is undoubtedly unusual; it seems that no other known Anglo-Saxon sites show the same combination of evidence for refuse disposal and the presence of exotic imports along with the complete lack of structural or routine residential evidence. However, such sites may not be as rare as the archaeological record suggests, and may already have been partially excavated, and interpreted as part of a more typical rural site. The nature of the activity at Dorney was only recognised due to the very large areas excavated. It would not have been easy to recognise the site for what it is if the areas opened up had been smaller, revealing just one or two isolated pits, as was the case with the initial evaluation of the site by means of small trenches. Equally the site was not recognised from field survey, and the relatively meagre assemblage of metalwork recovered means that metal-detecting would not have identified the area as a 'productive' site. Ultimately only time will tell whether the middle Saxon activity north of Dorney represents a unique phenomenon or an example of a new category of Anglo-Saxon temporary occupation sites.

Chapter 6:   The Medieval and Post-Medieval Archaeology

by Jonathan Hiller, Simon Mortimer, Tim Allen and Alan Hardy

Two of the main excavation sites on the Flood Alleviation Scheme (Lot's Hole and Lake End Road East) produced medieval stratigraphic evidence comprising successive phases of ditches and gullies defining fields and plots, a number of pits, mostly related by proximity to buildings, and the footprints of buildings defined by postholes and/or beam slots. Lake End Road West produced no securely datable medieval features.

Post-medieval evidence in the form of quarrying and structural features was confined almost exclusively to Lake End Road East, although at Lake End Road West some ditches were identified and dated, corresponding to field boundaries on old maps.

The medieval evidence from the Eton Rowing Course Project comprised a water hole and the surviving furrows of ridge- and-furrow cultivation. Environmental evidence suggested some hay meadows within a predominantly arable landscape.

Detailed descriptions of the medieval and post-medieval evidence from all these sites can be found in the appropriate sections of the CD-ROM. The evidence is summarised in this volume below.

SUMMARY OF THE STRATIGRAPHY
by Jonathan Hiller and Simon Mortimer

Lot's Hole (including the Gravel Storage Area) (Pl. 6.1)

Phasing (Fig. 6.1)

The phasing was determined by a combination of such stratigraphy as was investigated, artefactual dating, and perceived spatial relationships between individual features and groups of features. The middle Saxon pits were generally readily identifiable by their concentration, their size, and their artefactual contents. In contrast the medieval features (with a few exceptions) tended to produce artefact assemblages that did not allow close enough dating to determine phasing. The wide date-range of the principal medieval pottery fabrics, coupled with a high degree of residuality, meant that refined phasing by this means was unreliable. Where stratigraphic relationships between linear features did not exist (or were not confirmed) their size in profile, and alignment both to each other and to buildings were used to determine groups and ultimately construct a plausible sequence of phases. Pits tended to be clustered in groups – often in the vicinity of an individual building – leading to a reasonable assumption that the pit group and the building were associated.

Consequently, although the start and end dates, along with the first and last phases of activity of the medieval occupation are reasonably clear, the development of the intermediate phases (3 and 4) should be considered as plausible, not confirmable by the archaeological evidence. Some of the elements of Phase 3 may well belong to Phase 4 and vice versa. Consequently the phasing presented, and the precise dating of each phase, should be considered with caution.

Phase 2 (late 10th to 11th century) (Figs 6.1 & 6.2 no. 1)

The activity in this period was focused approximately 100 m north of the middle Saxon pits located at the southern end of the site, and between the palaeochannel to the west and the (probable) surviving trackway to the east.

The earliest phase was represented by a 1.7 m wide by 0.25 m deep ditch (51879/50477) oriented WSW-ENE, interrupted by a 1.0 m wide entrance. While the boundary formed by these two ditches was extant the entrance was closed off by a short curving gully (50113). The pottery from the silty clay ditch fills included material dating from the 10th–11th centuries and the 12th–14th centuries, although the later material is considered to be intrusive, and most probably derived from activity related to building 50664 (see below Phase 4).

Building 51993 (Fig. 6.3)

A concentrated spread of postholes (51993) was revealed immediately south of the boundary ditch 51879. The northern edge of the spread was approximately 3.0 m south of ditch 51879, and aligned parallel to it, which might suggest contemporaneity. The postholes appear to represent one or possibly two phases of building, although the exact form of such a building is unclear. Fragments of daub – possibly indicating the likely wall fabric – and the presence of charcoal and burnt flint were recorded in some of the posthole fills. The lack of an obviously coherent plan may indicate that the postholes represent two distinct structures, or one structure extensively rebuilt.

Droveway

An alignment of two interrupted and near-parallel ditches, situated approximately 90 m south of the boundary ditch, crossed the site, and possibly defined a droveway leading from the putative

Plate 6.1 Lot's Hole – during excavation – ditches in the foreground and the edge of the paleochannnel

north-south track off site to the east, to (and possibly beyond) the line of the palaeochannel which encroached onto the west side of the site. The two lines of ditches converged slightly to the west. Sample excavations of the features produced no dating material, and this, along with its early position in the sequence of linear ditches suggests that at the time the droveway ditches were open, it is unlikely that there has been intensive occupation nearby.

Phase 3 (early to mid 12th century) (Fig. 6.2)

The curved enclosure

The north-south division defined by the Phase 1 ditch was suppressed, and a curving enclosure was defined by four ditches (50564, 50782, 51500/51135 and 51884). Pottery from the enclosure dated to the 11th–13th centuries, although later material was also present in the northern part of the enclosure – this is taken to support the idea that part of the enclosure was reused in Phase 4. The west side of the enclosure was apparently open, possibly respecting the line of the north-south palaeochannel (see Fig. 2.1). The narrow NW-SE gully (51585) may have been an additional definition of this line. Two near-parallel ditches (50783 and 51156) extended eastwards out of the excavation area. Building 51880 was situated between the east ends of these two ditches.

Building 51880 (Fig. 6.3)

This was situated close to the east side of the enclosure ditch, and with similar orientation. Most of the eastern side of the building was truncated by later activity.

The building was defined by a series of beam slots with associated postholes, defining a rectangular structure measuring 8.0 m by 6.0 m, with two central aisle postholes (unexcavated) and three subsidiary internal roof supports inside the north-west, south-west and south-east corners. The west wall beam slot was interrupted, defining a 0.60 m wide entrance. Immediately west of the building were three pits, truncated by the later expansion of the enclosure.

Building 51452 was situated close to the south-east corner of the enclosure, where an interruption of the line of the enclosure may have defined an entrance.

Building 51452 (Fig. 6.3 & Pl. 6.2)

This was situated adjacent to the south side of ditch 51884. The building was defined by 32 postholes (3 unexcavated), interpreted as a rectangular structure measuring 7.0 m by 3.0 m, with external buttressing, at least on the west, east and south sides. No internal features were identified. Immediately north of the building was a large pit (51728) which contained a large quantity of animal bone (butchery refuse) and 11th–13th century pottery.

To the west of Building 51452 was a very shallow straight gully (51585), which extended north-west for 130 m. Its alignment appeared to be respecting the alignment of the building, and it may represent a nominal boundary, its orientation related to the eastern edge of the palaeochannel.

The water hole

Within the enclosure, and relatively isolated from any structure, was a large pit (50211), which may

Figure 6.1 Lot's Hole: all phases

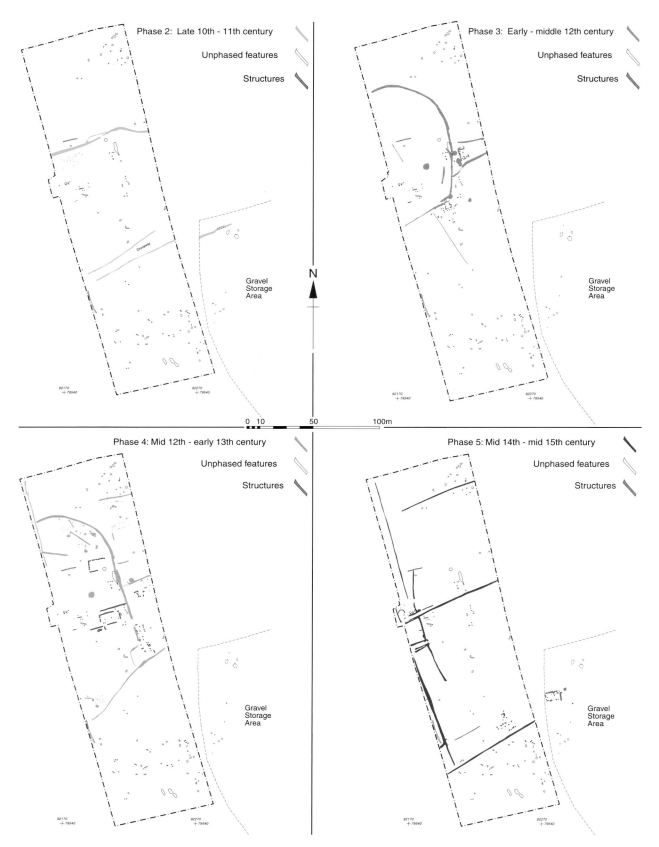

Figure 6.2   Lot's Hole: medieval phases

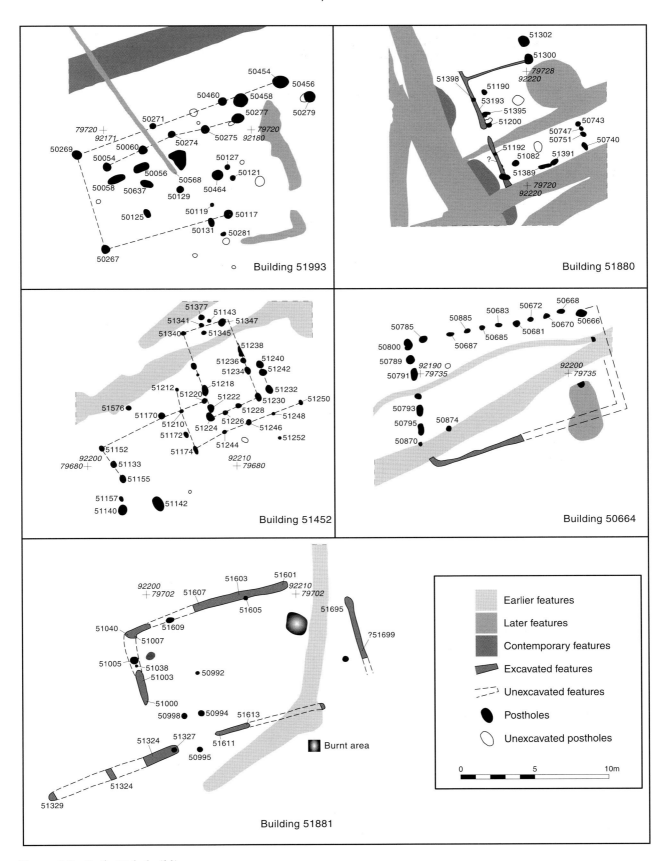

Figure 6.3   Lot's Hole buildings

Plate 6.2   Lot's Hole – during excavation – postholes of building 51452

have served as a water hole. The depth of the feature precluded full excavation of the lower fills on safety grounds. The date range of the pottery recovered from the upper fills of the feature (from early 12th century to the 14th century) suggests that the water hole may have been in use for the duration of the later occupation on the site.

Phase 4 (mid 12th to early 13th century)

The curved enclosure

The northern arc (50564) of the enclosure was maintained, while the southern part was extended to the south (ditches 50782, 51991 and 51854), increasing the total enclosed area by approximately 50%. A shallow north-south gully (50555) was identified alongside the western baulk, passing close to the north-west end of the enclosure. This may have been another defining boundary to the palaeochannel, performing a similar function to the Phase 3 ditch 51585.

Three buildings were identified within the enlarged enclosure.

Building 50664 (Fig. 6.3)

This was situated inside the northern part of the enclosure, overlying the original Phase 2 ditch. The building was defined by postholes and a beam slot representing three sides of a rectangular building measuring *c* 12.0 m by 8.5 m. The east wall and the eastern half of the south wall were truncated by later activity. Two internal roof-support postholes were identified, in a similar position to those found in

Building 51880. No other internal features were identified.

A series of ditches and pits were identified to the north and west of Building 50664. Only a few were subject to sample excavation, and the pottery from them ranged in date from the 11th to the 15th centuries. However, their distinct concentration within the arc of the enclosure leads to the conclusion that they were probably contemporary with this phase, and functionally associated with this structure.

Building 51881 (Fig. 6.3)

This was situated within the Phase 4 enclosure and on a similar orientation to Building 50664. The building was defined by a rectangular arrangement of interrupted beam slot gullies and postholes, in plan measuring 14.5 m by 9.0 m. A possible entrance 2.6 m wide, with one central exterior posthole and two internal postholes, was located close to the south-west corner. One definite and one possible ridge posthole were identified. Slight traces of burning identified within the building footprint suggest the possibility of domestic occupation. A small gully – possibly an eavesdrip – ran parallel to the north wall and linked to the enclosure ditch 50782. A short gully (51326) and three pits were situated close to the southern edge of the structure. A larger ditch (51712) was situated to the south, cutting the top of pit 51728 and (possibly) truncating the northern part of phase 3 building 51432. The fill of this ditch produced a quantity of 12th–15th century pottery.

Building 51597 (Fig. 6.4)

This was situated north of the south-western corner of the enclosure, close to the western edge of the site. The building was defined by 31 postholes interpreted as defining a rectangular building oriented NE-SW. The somewhat irregular scatter of internal postholes may imply at least one episode of rebuilding. Significant patches of decayed daub were identified to the north of the building, presumably derived from the wall fabric.

A further series of buildings was identified, situated outside the enclosure and possibly taking their alignment as much from the putative trackway as from the enclosure itself.

Building 52001 (Fig. 6.4)

Situated approximately 25 m north of the Phase 1 ditch 50477, this possible building was represented by 16 small and medium soil marks recorded on plan, but not excavated, since they were initially believed to be of natural origin. A few of the scatter of pits to the north of the structure were excavated, as was the possible boundary ditch (51335), producing a small quantity of pottery comprising residual 9th–10th century material and sherds from the 12th–13th century.

Building 52002 (Fig. 6.4)

This was situated south-east of Phase 3 Building 51880, although the precise relationship between the two was truncated by later activity. The building was defined by a concentration of 25 postholes, some of which suggest a structure measuring 4.7 m by 3.5 m, although the presence of other postholes which do not fit this pattern might indicate a sequence of structures of differing plan. A large pit (50968) and possible boundary ditch (51093) were situated a few metres to the north, and clearly truncated structure 51880. If the pit and ditch were associated with Building 52002, the absence of pottery might suggest that the structure did not function as a dwelling.

Two further buildings were located outside the south-eastern corner of the enlarged enclosure.

Building 51567 (Fig. 6.4)

This was situated immediately to the east of ditch 51991, and aligned with it. The building was defined by 13 postholes (5 unexcavated) representing a rectangular structure, oriented approximately north-south, and measuring 7.0 m by 5.5 m. Two of the postholes possibly represent internal ridge supports. A significant assemblage of 12th–13th century pottery was recovered from the ditch 51991, although this was considered to be residual material from truncated pit 51618.

Immediately to the south of the structure were five possible postholes which could represent an attached structure or a linking annex to building 51270 (see below).

Building 51270 (Fig. 6.4)

This was situated south of, and aligned with, Building 51567. The building was defined by 19 postholes (two unexcavated) interpreted as a rectangular structure 10.5 m by 4.5 m in plan. Two of the postholes possibly defined one side of an entrance porch on the west side of the building. An 'L'-shaped gully (51992) defined a small enclosed area, possibly a paddock or garden to the west of the building.

Phase 5 (mid 14th century to 15th century)

This phase is represented by a comprehensive reorganisation of the land division. The enlarged enclosure was abandoned, along with the focus of occupation and the associated buildings. Three NE-SW ditches (51889, 50679 and 51569) divided the area. The edge of the palaeochannel was again defined by a series of NW-SE ditches (51885, 51886 and 51888). A series of smaller ditches defined a possible paddock against the western edge of the site, close to a structure (50193).

Building 51826 (Fig. 6.5)

This was situated just north of the ditch 51889. It was defined by a spread of 14 soil marks, interpreted as probable postholes, possibly representing a rectangular building 9.0 m by 6.3 m, To the north of the building a further 8 postholes may represent an associated structure. No finds were recovered from the vicinity of the building, suggesting that it was a barn or byre, and did not function as an occupied domestic building.

Building X (Fig 6.5)

Within the Gravel Storage Area immediately east of the Lot's Hole excavation area, a concentration of 27 postholes and possible beam slots were observed in the watching brief, defining a rectangular structure approximately 13 m by 7 m. No context numbers were assigned to the postholes or to the structure they define; for the purpose of this report it is referred to as Building X. A row of five small postholes possibly represented a partition, dividing the interior into two unequal parts. Two internal postholes were identified in the western 'room'. Fragments of loomweight and burnt daub were recovered from the surface of one of the beam slots. No other features or finds were identified, and no clear dating material was recovered. On the basis of its proximity to Building 51826, the building is assigned to Phase 5.

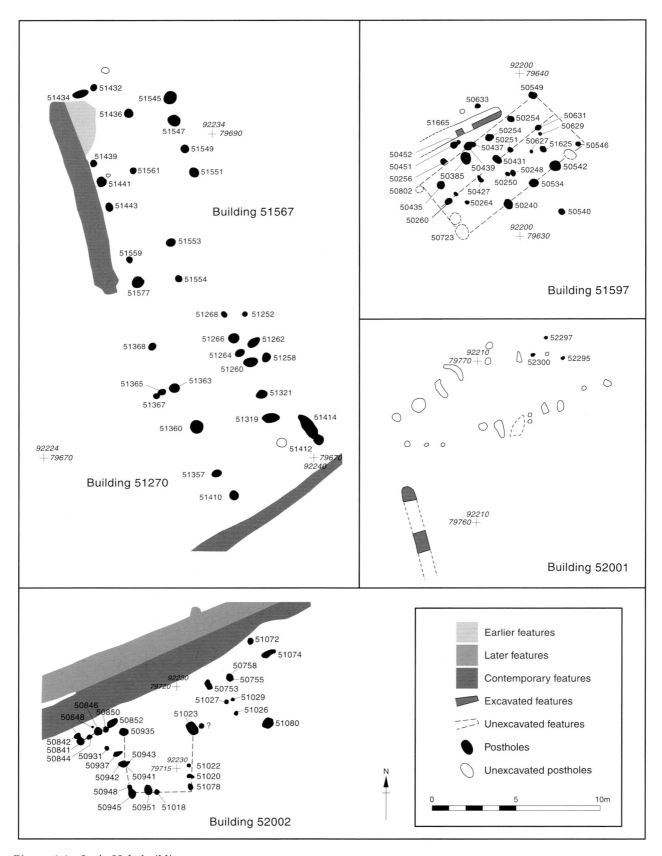

Figure 6.4   Lot's Hole buildings

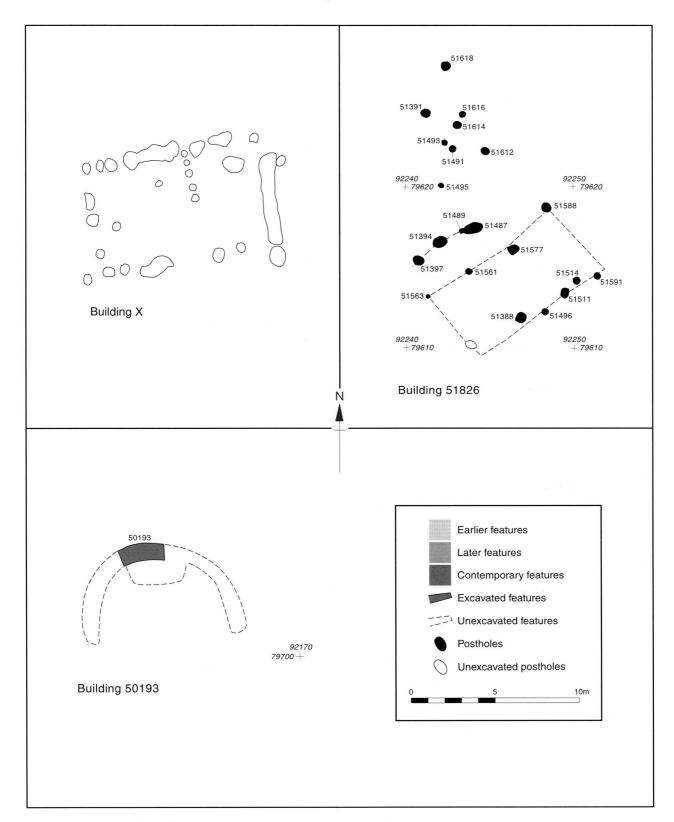

Figure 6.5   Lot's Hole buildings

Structure 50193 (Fig 6.5)

This was situated close to the west side of the site, and was represented by a vertically sided 0.5 m wide slot defining a precise semi-circle 4.9 m in diameter. The slot fill produced a mix of 11th–15th century pottery. The structure's function is not immediately obvious, though its situation on the edge of the palaeochannel to the west may be significant, implying an agricultural function – possibly a hay rick stand.

Lake End Road East *(Fig. 6.6)*

The analytical constraints apparent in the stratigraphic and artefactual evidence from this site were similar to those evident at Lot's Hole. The medieval phasing sequence is therefore offered as a hypothesis. In spite of this, in the context of the research priorities, a reasonable understanding of the broad development of the site has been achievable.

The medieval period

Chronology

While the pottery sequence from the site suggests a start date as early as the 10th century for occupation, virtually all of the late Saxon sherds were recovered from features also containing 11th–13th century pottery. Coupling this aspect with the uncertain stratigraphic sequence leads to severe difficulties in attempting to determine both the sequence and duration of enclosures, formed by the shallow ditches and gullies in the northern half of the site. Their similarity in size, linearity and disposition could suggest a consistent and unbroken pattern of land use, from the late 12th through to the late 14th century. All the enclosures broadly align north-south, presumably reflecting the alignment of the road or trackway west of the site. It is therefore reasonable to conclude that all the enclosures in some way relate to a succession of properties fronting the road.

Phase 2 (late 11th to mid 12th century)

The earliest medieval activity, as determined by the stratigraphy, was represented by three sides of a rectangular enclosure, the west and south sides defined by shallow gullies 30282 and 30782. No features within the enclosure were clearly associated, and only one sherd of (presumably intrusive) 13th-century pottery was recovered from the gully fills.

Phase 3 and 3a (possibly late 12th to possibly mid 13th century)

This phase saw the redefinition of the primary enclosure by a series of shallow gullies, and the extension of the arrangement of plot or field boundaries to the south, in the form of ditches 30795, 30796 and 30760. In the south-west corner a

concentration of postholes were identified, probably indicating a building. The dotted line on Figure 6.6 suggests a possible orientation and size for the structure, although no further evidence was recovered for its character, or indeed whether the postholes represent a single- or multiple-phase structure. Only a few of the postholes were excavated, and no associated dating evidence was recovered.

The building may be associated with the shallow ditched enclosure formed by ditches 30795, 30796, 30760, although the recovered dating material from associated features (ranging from prehistoric to postmedieval) emphasises the problems of residuality and intrusion.

Phase 4 (possibly mid to late 13th century)

A reorganisation of the local landscape is suggested by the laying out of a rectangular enclosure approximately 25 m east of the previous phase boundary ditches. The three ditches of this phase, 30781, 30787 and 30788 produced a small assemblage of pottery of 11th- to 13th-century date.

Phase 5 (14th to 16th century)

The flint lined pits (Pl. 6.3)

Close to the north-west corner of the enclosure were two rectangular pits, one of which (30441) cut through the Phase 3 ditch 30568/30789. Both were between 0.60 m and 0.80 m deep, with a flat base formed by compacted natural gravel. Both pits were lined with flint nodules and ceramic roofing tiles within a mortar matrix. The accumulated lower fills of the pits contained sequences of layers and/or lenses of grey/green silty clays, most of which contained high concentrations of mineralised wheat and fruit seeds (principally fig) and charcoal. Dating material from the lower layers comprised pottery dating from the 13th–16th centuries. The upper fills of both pits contained greater quantities of tile fragments, along with early post-medieval pottery and some residual 11th–13th century sherds. Among the finds from pit 30441 was a single amber bead, probably from a rosary.

No evidence was found of a superstructure over either pit, although, as it is likely that they were both earth closets or cess pits, any such superstructure would most probably have been insubstantial, and therefore truncated by more recent activity.

Pit 30570

A large subcircular pit was situated at the junction of Phase 3a ditches 30795 and 30796, and may have been contemporary with their use, originally functioning as a water hole. However, the material from the fills of the pit clearly demonstrate that by the end of the medieval period it was used as a rubbish pit, and also a convenient way of disposing of dead animals and butchery waste (see Chapter 7, Animal bone).

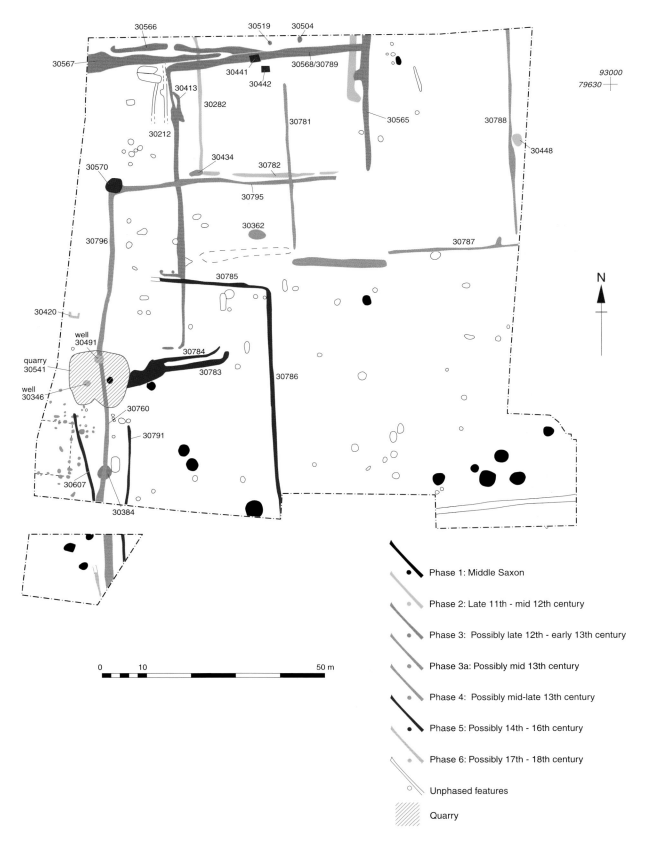

Figure 6.6   Lake End Road East: all phases

Phase 1: Middle Saxon

Phase 2: Late 11th - mid 12th century

Phase 3: Possibly late 12th - early 13th century

Phase 3a: Possibly mid 13th century

Phase 4: Possibly mid-late 13th century

Phase 5: Possibly 14th - 16th century

Phase 6: Possibly 17th - 18th century

Unphased features

Quarry

Plate 6.3   Lake End Road East – flint-lined pit 30441

Quarry pit

In the south-west quadrant of the site, a backfilled quarry pit (30541) was identified, measuring approximately 9 m by 9 m by at least 1.4 m deep. Its edge had eroded while the pit was open so that the total area disturbed by the quarry's excavation was close to 200 sq m. The backfill of the pit was a sequence of lenses of sandy gravels and sandy loams, producing pottery of the 16th–17th century, along with some sherds of a 14th–16th century fabric.

Quarry enclosure, track and approach

Leading east from the quarry area were two parallel features (30783 and 30784) which could represent gullies bordering a track, in use during the quarry's operation.

The quarry and the track were bounded to the north and east by an enclosure (ditches 30785 and 30786) from which a single sherd of 14th–16th century pottery was recovered. Two shallow gullies (30607 and 30791) approached the southern side of the quarry area from the southern baulk. They may well define an approach or track contemporary with the quarry's operation, although neither feature produced any dating material.

Phase 6 (17th to 18th century)

Two wells were located (30491 and 30346), dug into the backfill of the quarry pit; both were excavated to an approximate depth of 1.2 m. The lower shaft of well 30491 was lined with a hollowed-out tree trunk, surmounted by a lining of rough chalk blocks and flint nodules. Pottery recovered from the accumulated backfills predominantly dated to the 16th–18th centuries. The lower shaft of well 30346 was also lined with a square wooden frame (30769), the upper part of which was exposed (see Pl. 6.4). The upper part of the well shaft appeared to have been of a similar construction to that of 30491 – chalk block and flint – but had been heavily disturbed and robbed by later activity. The backfills of the well contained 17th- and 18th-century pottery along with fragments of brick and tile.

The disturbed remains of an insubstantial brick and rubble structure (30420), surviving to a depth of 0.10 m (one brick course) was identified approximately 10 m north-west of well 30491. It measured approximately 2.0 m by 1.5 m in plan and was roughly U-shaped in plan. The mortared brick and rubble lay upon a bed of mortar with traces of burning. No dating evidence was recovered, although the size of the bricks (as estimated from the fragments) suggest an 18th- or 19th-century date. The structure appears to represent a small fireplace, possibly a rudimentary garden incinerator.

Lake End Road West

A number of ditches were identified across the site (see Fig. 5.1) which in some cases cut individual Saxon pits and/or the Romano-British features. Some of the ditches were traceable on maps of the area. The fills of the ditches were uniformly dark brown loamy silt. Selective excavation produced residual material and a small quantity of late medieval or post-medieval material in the form of tile fragments, 17th-18th century pottery and a few

Plate 6.4   Lake End Road East – well-lining 30346

coins. Generally the assemblage supports the contention that this area was open agricultural land from the medieval period onwards.

The Eton Rowing Course project *(Fig. 1.4)*
by Tim Allen

A single medieval water hole or pond (11111) was identified close to Boveney (see Fig. 6.7). The water hole contained evidence of overbank flooding, and alluvium was also recorded overlying Roman ditches in Area 20 at the north-west end of the site (see Chapter 7). Examination of the alluvial sequence over the former palaeochannels and flood-plain showed further evidence of post-Roman alluviation, but it was not possible to date this clearly. The alluvium in Area 20 was cut through by a curving ditch (15005) mirroring the shape of the largely silted Channel N to the east, and following

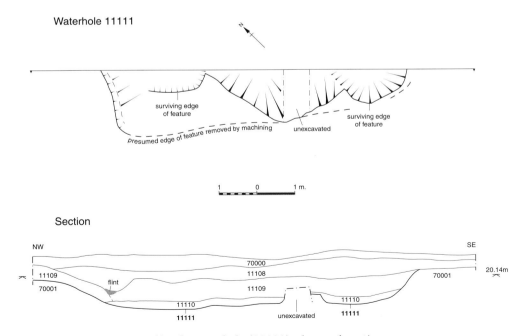

Figure 6.7   Eton Rowing Course. Medieval water hole (11111) plan and section

the approximate boundary between the lower-lying ground with alluvium and the higher gravel terrace to the west (see Fig. 1.4). This feature contained fragments of two horseshoes, one of 13th/14th century type, indicating a late-medieval or post-medieval date.

Across the whole study area the archaeological evidence was solely agricultural and environmental. Excavation in Areas 10 and 24 revealed the furrows of ridge-and-furrow cultivation, visible in the latter case on aerial photographs. Further traces of ridge-and-furrow were found in Area 6. Field-walking over Area 6 showed a spread of medieval and post-medieval pottery and tile, presumably manuring from the hamlet of Boveney just to the north.

Chapter 7: Medieval and Post-Medieval Finds and Environmental Evidence

FINDS – SUMMARY REPORTS

Full reports on the finds, including catalogues and illustrations, can be found on the CD-ROM. This volume contains summary reports and selected illustrations.

The pottery *(Figs 7.1–2)*
by Lucy Whittingham

At Lake End Road East a large proportion of the assemblage dates through from Saxo-Norman to post-medieval (6% Saxo-Norman, 32% early medieval, 14% medieval and 37% post-medieval). The pottery from phased contexts corresponds closely to the archaeological features with little sign of disturbance or residuality. In comparison to Lake End Road East the ceramic assemblage at Lot's Hole is more limited with fewer fabric types ranging over a shorter time span. It can be summarised as 12% Saxo-Norman, 72% early medieval, 3% medieval, 0.2% post-medieval and has a high degree of residuality.

Saxo-Norman pottery

At Lot's Hole a collection of Saxo-Norman fabrics (F9, 10, 12, 13, 14 and 15), although mostly residual, are indicative of late 9th- to 11th-century activity on the site (see Fig. 7.1 nos 1, 2 & 3). They are dated as Saxo-Norman by comparison with other Saxo-Norman wares, such as a chalk-tempered ware (Fabric C2) at Wraysbury (Astill and Lobb 1989) and fabrics MD2 and MD3a at the Friends Burial Ground, Staines (Jones 1984). Only Fabrics 14 and 15 occurred at Lake End Road East.

Late Saxon to early medieval pottery

Lake End Road East

The 10th- to early 12th-century phase of activity at Lake End Road East is represented in the ceramic sequence by Fabrics 11, 14 and 15. The majority of these sherds (57 of 69) appeared to be redeposited – occurring in medieval phase 3a and phase 4 contexts which also produced late 11th to 13th century (Fabric 18) material. Fabric 15 can be paralleled at Wraysbury by the late Saxon Fabric D4 (ibid. 1989). Fabric 11 can be paralleled by a 12th-century fabric at the site of Bierton, near Aylesbury (Whittingham 1997). Fabric 14 has no parallels but produces slashed rod handles and cooking vessels of an early medieval style.

Early medieval pottery

Lake End Road East

Fabric 18 is the principal early medieval fabric in the Lake End Road East assemblage, accounting for 60% of the early medieval wares (Fig. 7.1 nos 7–8, Fig. 7.2 no. 9). It is quite possible that Fabric 18 is a local product to Dorney, but produced within a more widespread late 11th to early 13th-century greyware tradition. This earlier medieval date is considered to be more appropriate to its context within the Lake End Road East site. This fabric produces a wide range of wheel-thrown grey quartz-tempered cooking pots and jugs which are common in many features of medieval period 4 (ditches 30760, 30207, 30808, 30567, post-pipe 30247, and pits 30261, 30358, 30360, 30384, 30488, 30504, 30519, 30570, and flint-lined pits 30441 and 30442), but the larger quantities occur particularly in pits 30384, 30504, 30507, flint lined pits 30441 and 30442 and ditch 30760. There are 44 large sherds, weighing 1.5 kg, from the same decorated jug (Fig. 7.2 no. 9) in flint-lined pit 30441, contexts 30581 and 30582.

A second early medieval ware, Fabric 16 occurs as one sherd in pit 30257. This fabric has the characteristic red iron-stained quartz of mid 11th- to mid 12th-century Early Surrey Ware but is also similar to the description of an Ironstone-tempered Ware at the Friends Burial Ground, Staines (Fabric MK4, Jones 1984) where it is dated to the mid 13th to mid 14th century.

Lot's Hole

The early medieval assemblage at Lot's Hole is represented by Fabrics 16, 17 and 18 (see Fig. 7.1 nos 4, 5 & 6). As similar proportions of each fabric occur in all sub-phases it is not possible to distinguish from the stratigraphy which fabrics might be earlier or later in date. Fabric 18 is the major type occurring in similar percentages in all three phases. Fabrics 16 and 17 occur in small groups of less than twenty sherds in all three phases. Fabrics 16 and 18 are suggested as 11th- to mid 13th-century wares and Fabric 17 slightly later, 12th to 15th century.

Regionally imported medieval wares

Lake End Road East

Part of this assemblage consisted of 133 early and late medieval 'established wares', of which the majority (83 sherds) are associated with contexts in phase 4. Seven sherds of early 12th-century Coarse London-type Ware are the earliest of these wares,

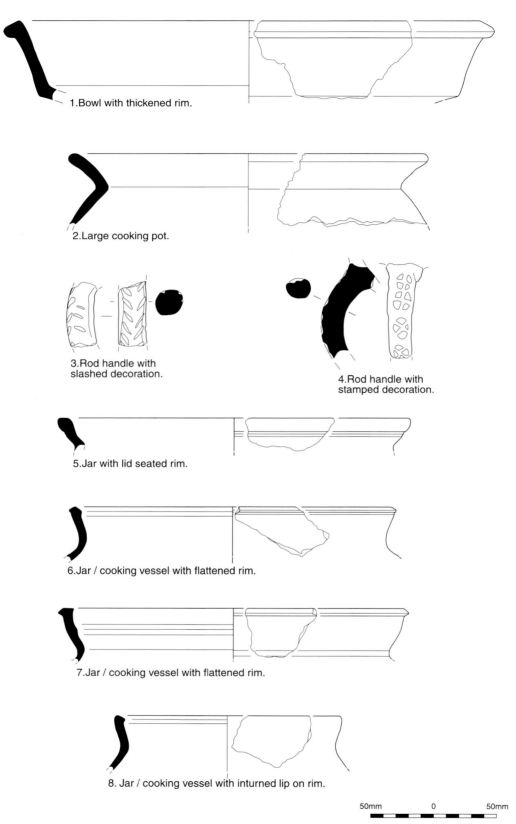

1.Bowl with thickened rim.

2.Large cooking pot.

3.Rod handle with slashed decoration.

4.Rod handle with stamped decoration.

5.Jar with lid seated rim.

6.Jar / cooking vessel with flattened rim.

7.Jar / cooking vessel with flattened rim.

8. Jar / cooking vessel with inturned lip on rim.

50mm   0   50mm

Figure 7.1   Pottery 1–8

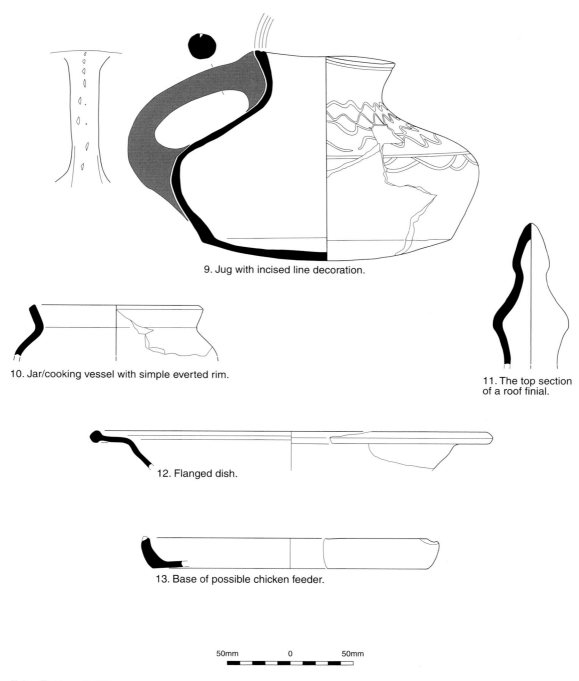

9. Jug with incised line decoration.

10. Jar/cooking vessel with simple everted rim.

11. The top section of a roof finial.

12. Flanged dish.

13. Base of possible chicken feeder.

50mm   0   50mm

Figure 7.2   Pottery 9–13

found in ditch 30707. The late medieval 'established wares' include a mid 13th to mid 15th century London-type Ware roof finial, 68 sherds of mid 13th to mid 14th century Kingston-type Ware, 2 sherds of mid 14th- to mid 15th-century Cheam Whiteware and 6 sherds of mid 14th- to mid 16th-century Coarse Border ware. With the exception of pit 30570 which contains nearly all of the Kingston-type Ware sherds these late medieval 'established wares' appear to be distributed in different features from the Saxo-Norman and early medieval coarse-wares (Fabrics 11, 14, 15 and 18). The Cheam Whiteware is in well 30491 and pit 30570 and the Coarse Border Ware in pits 30362, 30434 and 30442, ditch 30780 and posthole 30598. It appears that both the early and later medieval established wares, which represent the purchasing of marketed goods from Surrey and London, are found in different contexts from the local coarsewares in period 4.

Very few sherds of 'established wares' occurred at Lot's Hole, and these were intrusive material in earlier features.

Post-medieval pottery

Lake End Road East

The majority of the post-medieval pottery belongs to two types of fine and coarse Red Earthenware, a Slipware and a Blackware all dating from the mid 16th to mid 18th centuries (Fig. 7.2 nos 12, 13). The post-medieval assemblage consists of small quantities of late 14th- to mid 16th-century Tudor Green ware, late 15th- and 16th-century Rhenish Stoneware drinking jugs, mid 16th- to mid 18th-century Surrey Hampshire Border wares and 18th-century Staffordshire White Glazed Stoneware, Tin Glazed Earthenware and English Porcelain. There is no distinction in the occurrence of the earlier and later post medieval pottery on the site. All are associated in quantity with quarry pit 30541 and wells 30491 and 30346 and unphased contexts 30089 and 30130.

Conclusion

Both the Lake End Road East and the Lot's Hole assemblages fit into the local pattern of pottery production for this part of the Thames Valley. Both assemblages are similar in the types of fabrics present but vary in date range. Lake End Road East has a greater range of fabrics, ranging from the medieval to post-medieval periods, whilst Lot's Hole has a greater range of Saxo-Norman fabrics and no post-medieval pottery. The Saxon assemblages at both sites are particularly well preserved. They are typical and comparable with other assemblages in the area, for example, Wraysbury (Astill and Lobb 1989), Old Windsor (Wilson and Hurst 1958) and Staines (Jones and Moorhouse 1981 and Jones 1984). The residual Saxo-Norman assemblage at Lot's Hole is of interest as it may relate to some of the post and trench buildings on the site. Both medieval assemblages contain mainly local coarse cooking pots and relatively few jugs. There are few large groups of sherds associated with particular features at either site and consequently the assemblages are rather ubiquitous throughout every medieval phase.

At Lake End Road East the later medieval 'established wares' occur within the same phase but in different contexts from the early medieval coarsewares, possibly serving different functions. The greater quantity of these 'established wares' and early post-medieval regional and continental Rhenish imports is indicative of a stable settlement in contact with local trading markets. The mid 13th- to mid 15th-century roof finial also suggests that there was a building of some quality on the site at this date.

The small amount of imported 'established wares' at Lot's Hole by comparison suggests that occupation could have ceased by the late 14th century, and

was not oriented towards regional trade networks in the same way as Lake End Road East.

The post-medieval assemblage at Lake End Road East contains a standard range of wares for the 16th–18th centuries with a few additional late 18th-century products.

Gravel Storage Area

Medieval pottery

Four of the medieval sherds recovered were of a fabric not previously found at Lake End Road or Lot's Hole (context 23). These are coarsely tempered sherds with shelly limestone/calcareous, quartz and red iron ore temper. One sherd is diagnostic and clearly from a simple everted jar rim. The fabric and form are indicative of a Saxo-Norman date *c* 1050–1150. Other medieval sherds are typical of kiln products from Camley Gardens, near Henley (Pike 1965), and one was similar to a Surrey Whiteware, dating from 1350–1500.

Post-medieval pottery

A scatter of mainly 17th- to 19th-century sherds was recovered.

The Eton Rowing Course project

Thirty one medieval sherds were recovered from all of the investigated areas. The majority of these were small sherds in a ubiquitous quartz tempered fabric (Fabric 18) similar to Oxford Fabric OXY (Mellor 1994) dated late 11th- mid 13th-century or to the material from Camley Gardens Estate kiln site near Maidenhead (Pike 1965) dated 13th to early 16th century. The difficulty in dating such 'local' wares is compounded here by the small size of all the sherds which are nearly all undiagnostic. One cooking pot rim in context 6749 is a simple everted form with internal bevelled edge similar to a late 13th- to mid 14th-century cooking pot form found in Surrey Whiteware; Kingston-type ware (Pearce and Vince 1988, fig. 94 no. 296).

Other fabrics included Fabric 15, which is represented by four large sherds from a rounded hand-built jug with short everted rim and stabbed rod handle from a pond or water hole (11111) in Area 6. This vessel can be paralleled at Lake End Road East (Fig. 7.1 no. 3) where it was found in contexts containing late 13th- to mid 16th-century material.

Other diagnostic medieval sherds occur in Surrey Whitewares: Kingston-type ware and Coarse Border ware. Twenty-two sherds in Kingston-type ware are copper glazed sherds from small late 14th-century biconical jugs and bowls (ibid. 1988, fig. 83 nos 205–6). The three Coarse Border ware sherds are undiagnostic.

Early post-medieval wares occur primarily in local red earthenware and slipware products of the 17th and early 18th century. Regionally imported wares include an 18th century Tin Glazed Earthenware chamber pot and two sherds of late 16th- to 17th-century Surrey Hampshire Border ware and Staffordshire White Salt Glazed Stoneware.

Late 18th- to 19th-century wares include English Stoneware bottles, Transfer Printed Wares, Creamware, Pearlware, Red Stoneware, Yellow ware, Chinese and English Porcelain and Refined White Earthenware.

Pottery from fieldwalking in Area 6

Students from Reading University walked part of Area 6 during the late spring of 1995 and recovered a variety of post-medieval pottery and tile, the vast majority consisting of red earthenwares dating from the 17th-19th centuries. The students' report upon the pottery from fieldwalking is held in the archive.

The metalwork *(Fig. 7.3)*
by Ian Scott and Leigh Allen

Methodology

The objects were attributed broad functional categories for the purposes of analysis, for example: tools, dress items and household or domestic items. As the number and range of objects are small, the validity of any discussion of the numbers or proportions of objects in any functional category is limited.

The unstratified objects have been omitted from the published catalogue, except where they can be identified either as medieval or early post-medieval on typological grounds. Unidentified fragments have also been omitted. Stratified nails and miscellaneous pieces of sheet, bar, etc have been tabulated by context.

Lot's Hole

The metalwork assemblage from Lot's Hole is not large, and is predominantly of later medieval or post-medieval date. There were 72 iron objects or fragments, 30 copper alloy objects and 25 lead objects. A shield-shaped heraldic pendant (Fig. 7.3 no. 4) from an early medieval context is certainly later medieval in date and intrusive. Such pendants are usually dated to the 14th century, although the earliest appear to be dated to the 12th century (Griffiths 1986). The finger ring (Fig. 7.3 no. 1), buckle frame (Fig. 7.3 no. 2) and annular buckle (Fig. 7.3 no. 3) are medieval. The other pieces are not closely datable. The copper alloy is limited in range and domestic or personal in character.

The ironwork assemblage was dominated by nails (37 items) and miscellaneous pieces of rod, bar, sheet and strip (18 items). Most of this material comes from contexts dated by pottery to the medieval period.

There were two heckle teeth and a knife. The remaining identifiable ironwork comprises a needle, a lever lock key (Fig. 7.3 no. 5), a horseshoe fragment, and nails, a possible knife blade fragment, and a U-shaped staple and a hook.

Lake End Road East

The metalwork assemblage from Lake End Road East was not especially large. There were 153 iron objects or fragments, but only 18 copper alloy objects and 5 lead fragments. Three of the objects from medieval contexts came from the lower fills of flint-lined pit 30441, which contained medieval pottery: two heavily corroded tacks with circular domed heads (SF 32106, context 30582), and a small mount, or edge binding, curved in section with two tiny circular rivet holes (SF 32102, context 30581). Another tack with a slightly domed head circular (SF 32099, context 30556) came from the upper fill of the same flint-lined pit. The pottery from the pit ranges in date from the 13th century to the early post-medieval period.

The post-medieval finds include a buckle plate from a fill of a post-medieval well 30491. A selection of pins was recovered from various medieval and post-medieval contexts. The two unstratified copper alloy objects comprise a cast ring (SF 32136) and a cast terminal or foot in the form of a hoof with horseshoe.

The ironwork assemblage although bigger, comprised largely nails (64) and miscellaneous fragments (20), most of which were from post-medieval or modern contexts, and have not been catalogued. Among the other material were a hinge strap (Fig. 7.3 no. 7) and a small figure-of-eight hasp (Fig. 7.3 no. 6), both from the basal fill of flint-lined pit 30441, and both dating to between the 13th and 16th centuries.

The objects from post-medieval contexts, none of which are catalogued, included a smith's punch, and a boat-hook. Also recovered was a table fork with two tines and a 'pistol-grip' wooden handle (Fig. 7.3 no. 8).

Lake End Road West

The metalwork assemblage from Lake End Road West was not especially large, but its composition is interesting. There were 140 iron objects or fragments, 67 copper alloy objects and 35 lead fragments.

Most of the copper alloy assemblage (59 of 67 objects) including 25 buttons, a hatpin head, a drawing pin head and a half a cufflink derives from topsoil (40001) and is of late post-medieval date. The identifiable early post-medieval finds include a small number of personal items; buckles, a clothing hook and a cast pellet bell.

In contrast to the copper alloy assemblage, very little of the ironwork assemblage can be confidently ascribed to the medieval or post-medieval period on typological or stratigraphic grounds, except a few pieces of undistinguished scraps or obviously modern wire nails recovered from the topsoil.

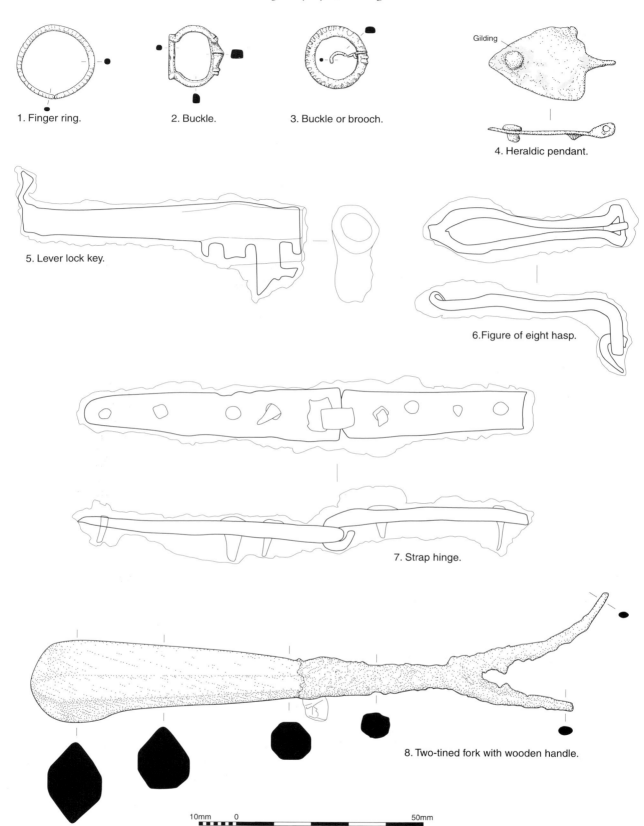

1. Finger ring.

2. Buckle.

3. Buckle or brooch.

Gilding

4. Heraldic pendant.

5. Lever lock key.

6. Figure of eight hasp.

7. Strap hinge.

8. Two-tined fork with wooden handle.

10mm   0   50mm

Figure 7.3   Medieval and post-medieval metalwork and ironwork 1–8

Discussion

Lot's Hole

The metalwork assemblage from Lot's Hole is small, and dominated by medieval and early post-medieval domestic or personal items. The copper alloy assemblage includes several medieval pieces, including a shield pendant (Fig. 7.3 no. 4) and small buckle frame (Fig. 7.3 no. 2). A finger ring (Fig. 7.3 no. 1) and small annular buckle (Fig. 7.3 no. 3) are also probably medieval.

The shield-shaped pendant belongs to a class of object identified by Griffiths (1986; 1989; 1995) and dated to the late 13th or 14th century. The small buckle frame is a typical medieval find and widely paralleled, for example at Norwich (Margeson 1993, fig. 13 no. 131) and London (Egan and Pritchard 1993, 72, fig. 44 nos 295, 300). The annular buckle, or brooch, is paralleled in London (Egan and Pritchard 1991, figs 160, 162) and Norwich (Margeson 1993, fig. 7 no. 56). The finger ring is not precisely paralleled, but similarly decorated rings have been found in London (Egan and Pritchard 1993, fig. 217 nos 1627, 1629).

The iron assemblage was particularly small and undistinguished, consisting principally of domestic waste, horseshoe nails and knife fragments. The lead, which was largely unstratified, comprised mainly offcuts.

Lake End Road East

The assemblage from Lake End Road East was dominated by ironwork. The few copper alloy objects include a buckle plate from an early post-medieval context. The other copper alloy objects included corroded tacks, a small fragment of a binding and pins.

The medieval iron material comprised a range of domestic equipment, although the assemblage is too small to draw any firm conclusions, although it is worth noting that the hasp and strap hinge (Fig. 7.3 nos 6 and 7) may originate from the same medieval casket.

The objects from post-medieval contexts, none of which is catalogued, include a smith's punch, and a set or punch, a boat-hook and worn horseshoe. There are fragments of two 18th-century shoe buckles and a table fork with two tines and a 'pistol-grip' wooden handle (Fig. 7.3 no. 8). The handle is facetted and attached to the fork by a whittle tang. The stem of the fork is decorated with a baluster moulding. Table forks were introduced into Britain in the 17th century and were not widely used until late in the century. The baluster moulding was common before the later 18th century, and the pistol grip was an 18th-century feature (Noël Hume 1991, 177–80).

Lake End Road West

No significant metalwork or ironwork finds were recovered from this site.

The Eton Rowing Course project
by Leigh Allen

The material was largely retrieved during metal-detecting of the topsoil and spoilheaps and as such is unstratified. The vast majority is of post-medieval or modern date. The few items of intrinsic interest included two arms from two separate horseshoes – both from context 15678 in ditch 15005 in Area 20. One of the arms (SF 93037) can be dated with reasonable confidence to the 13th–14th century (Clark 1995, type 3, 86–7, fig. 83.850).

ECOFACTUAL AND ENVIRONMENTAL EVIDENCE – SUMMARY

Detailed reports on the medieval and post-medieval ecofactual and environmental evidence can be found in the appropriate sections of the CD-ROM.

The animal bone
by Adrienne Powell

The medieval material from Lot's Hole is largely of late-13th century date, while the material from Lake End Road East spans the 11th–16th centuries and has been divided into medieval (up to mid 14th century) and late medieval (post mid 14th century). No animal bone from contexts datable to the medieval period was recovered from Lake End Road West. Most aspects of the two assemblages are discussed separately by site, although livestock size is considered for both sites together to facilitate comparison between the two sites and with other sites.

Lot's Hole

The medieval assemblage comprised 2699 fragments of which 24% were identified to species. Most of the identified bone (92%, excluding skeletons) derived from domestic mammals.

Relative abundance of the main domestic mammals

In contrast to the Saxon assemblage, pig bones predominate, followed in frequency by cattle bones. Sheep bones are relatively poorly represented. Horse and dog bones are present although the latter are rare, and domestic fowl is the most common bird in both assemblages. A range of wild species is present, occurring in very small numbers.

It is possible that the apparent change in species representation between the Saxon and medieval phases is the result of spatial variation in the distribution of bone and change in the types of features from which bone was recovered. In contrast to the Saxon assemblage which was almost entirely recovered from pits, the medieval assemblage comes mainly from ditches (61% of the hand retrieved bone), with pits contributing less than half of this amount and a minimal contribution from other feature types. However, examination of the proportion of species-types in varying features established that the difference was minimal, and changes in the numbers of identified species (NISP), minimum number of elements and minimum number of individuals figures between the Saxon and medieval phases are better interpreted as change in the preferred species on site, rather than a consequence of different features having been sampled.

Body part representation and butchery

It was suggested above that cattle and pig might be represented to a greater degree by complete carcasses than sheep. The patterns for all three species are very similar to those of the Saxon assemblage and suggest that this assemblage is largely derived from the original presence on site of whole carcasses, which were then butchered, rather than the importation of already butchered joints.

Although there is much less butchery evidence than in the Saxon assemblage, the bones do show all stages of carcass processing: skinning, division of the carcass, removal of the flesh and horn working, even a few long bones showing longitudinal splitting for marrow. The few vertebrae in the medieval assemblage show transverse processes chopped from the ventral surface indicating, as in the Saxon material, that carcasses were split into sides in a sagittal plane probably while the animal was lying on the ground.

Far fewer sheep bones were butchered than cattle, but bones show evidence of disjointing and filleting, with one horn core showing chop marks from removal of the horn sheath. Butchered pig bones are also uncommon, and appear to be mostly the result of disjointing the carcass.

Age and sex of the main domestic mammals

There is a high proportion of mature bones compared to immature bones present for cattle and sheep, while the proportions are closer for pig.

For cattle, it seems that few animals were killed before the end of their fourth year, although there is a suggestion that the kill-off may have started in the third year, so there is a little evidence for younger deaths, and it seems that most animals survived into adulthood and even to old age. This pattern suggests that the main role of cattle in the economy at this site was as providers of traction, or dairying.

Most of the sheep bones are fused and there is no evidence for any animals being killed before reaching their second year but there is almost no evidence for the older juvenile and mature individuals. The tooth eruption data provide more detail on these animals with most mandibles coming from animals killed between one and four years of age and two of the nine ageable jaws coming from animals surviving into old age. This pattern may be interpreted as an indication of wool production and is not unexpected for a rural site.

From their epiphyseal fusion data, pigs appear to have been killed in their second year but there are no late-fusing bones present and so little evidence of older animals. However, it appears from the dental data that many animals did survive longer: the adult mandibles all had their third molars in the early stages of wear, suggesting these animals were slaughtered in their third year.

Other domestic mammals

Horse is the only mammal apart from cattle, sheep and pig which is present in significant numbers. Its bones comprise 8% of the total NISP for domestic mammals in the medieval assemblage, representing a minimum of three individuals; this includes a series of articulating vertebrae (context 51208). Some of the bone showed butchery marks which could have resulted from either dismembering or stripping meat from the bone. Butchered horse bone is not rare, even on medieval sites (eg Jennings Yard, Bourdillon 1993; Faccombe, Sadler 1990 and Launceston Castle, Albarella and Davis 1994). The most likely explanation for the marks is that horse carcasses were butchered and fed to dogs.

There is no evidence within the bone assemblage for the breeding of horses at the site: only nine bones retained information on the state of epiphyseal fusion and all are fused. The youngest age estimate from cheek tooth crown heights is three to six and a half years on a maxillary tooth; most of the others came from animals who were probably still of working age, although there was one older animal in the group.

Only one specimen of dog occurred in this assemblage, a mandible from ditch context 50479, with measurements that suggest that the animal could have been very similar to a modern greyhound. Of particular interest is a fine knife mark on the mandible, very close to the ventral surface below the second molar. Knife marks in series on this aspect of Iron Age dog mandibles have been previously interpreted as the result of removal of the tongue (Powell and Clark 1996). Whether this operation could be carried out so as to leave only a single fine cut on the bone is debatable, but it is difficult to suggest any other reason for a cut in this region, unless it is associated with skinning.

Wild mammals

As in the Saxon assemblage, the most common wild mammal species was roe deer (*Capreolus capreolus*), almost entirely represented by antler parts and limb bones, suggesting a characteristic origin, namely the spoils from a kill site elsewhere. The presence of deer in a medieval assemblage is generally said to indicate a relatively high status site (Grant 1988). However given that the manor of Dorney, in which Lot's Hole is located, contained woodland, at least at the time of the Domesday survey, the possibility of poaching cannot be ruled out.

Birds

The most commonly represented bird was the domestic fowl (*Gallus gallus*), including a substantially complete skeleton (context 51717, pit 51760) of a mature hen bird. Other bird species were poorly represented by a few goose and duck bones.

Lake End Road East

The total number of fragments in the assemblage was 1376 (excluding the skeletons from pit 30570), with 14% identifiable to species. Most of the material comes from medieval groups, with only a few fragments of horse, cattle, sheep and pig coming from late medieval/post-medieval deposits. The latter group is not discussed further.

Most of the identifiable bone (92%) is from the domestic mammals of which pig is the most frequently occurring species, followed by cattle then sheep. Horse, dog and cat were present. Domestic fowl is the most commonly occurring bird. A limited range of wild species is represented. Most of the identifiable bone in the medieval assemblage derives from several complete or partially complete skeletons of various domestic species which had been deposited in a single pit.

Evidence of butchery occurred at a low level, with chop marks being more frequent than knife cuts. Both gnawing and butchery marks occurred at a lower level than in the Saxon phase. The amount of butchered bone (excluding skeletons) is similar to Lot's Hole but the frequency of gnawed bone is higher at Lot's Hole.

Pit 30570

This single feature produced over half of the medieval bone at Lake End Road East (1090 hand retrieved and 395 sieved fragments) and contained all but one of the skeletons which dominate the medieval assemblage. The skeletons present included:

1) A partial horse skeleton (context 30619), of an adult male probably around seven years old. Fine knife cuts on the skull are interpreted as evidence of skinning. No other butchery evidence is present, although the absence of major parts of the skeleton indicates that the carcass was dismembered before being dumped in this pit.
2) The substantially complete skeletons of two calves (contexts 30656, 30704, 30705, 30767), including cranial elements, most of the vertebrae, some ribs, and the limb bones. Neither of these skeletons showed any evidence of butchery or pathology.
3) A partial dog skeleton recovered entirely from context 30704, apart from four phalanges, a metatarsal and three tarsal bones from context 30656. Unfortunately there is no cranial material, but the single mandible is robust and well formed and compares metrically with modern compara-

tive dimensions of Alsatian and Labrador, as do the pelvis, sacrum and forelimb bones. The pelvis had fine cut marks on the ventral surface of the right ischium, and further fine cut marks were visible on the shaft of the left ulna. These suggest disarticulation rather than skinning and therefore indicate butchery for meat consumption.
4) Two partial cat skeletons from contexts 30704, 30656 and possibly 30569, with both animals represented by cranial, trunk and limb bones.

Other mammals

Horse bones are present in small numbers in the medieval and late medieval material, and excluding the partial skeleton comprise 13% of the domestic mammals in the medieval group. The partial horse skeleton has been described in detail above. The remainder of the medieval assemblage includes elements from the skull, trunk and limbs. These and the partial skeleton indicate that whole carcasses were present on the site, although they were not buried as such.

Birds

Domestic fowl is the most frequent species; the bones present are from at least two individuals although these are represented entirely by limb bones. This pattern is probably the result of a survival bias. Pigeon (*Columba sp.*), absent from the Lot's Hole assemblage, occurs here as four tarsometatarsi which represent at least three individuals, all of whom were immature. This suggests that the bones could have come from domestic birds, although their domestic or wild status could not be determined from measurements. A few goose and duck bones were also recovered

Discussion

While the medieval assemblages from Lot's Hole and Lake End Road East can be usefully considered together in relation to the Saxon assemblage from both sites and Lake End Road West, few meaningful conclusions can be drawn from directly comparing the medieval assemblages, given the differing excavation strategies and the derivation of a large proportion of the Lake End Road East assemblage from a single feature.

Comparable sizes of the domestic animals in the Saxon and medieval periods

Comparison of the Saxon and medieval cattle metatarsals suggests that there was no change in size of animals at Lot's Hole and Lake End Road East between the Saxon and medieval phases.

Comparison of sheep distal tibia suggests that Saxon sheep may have been slightly larger than the medieval sheep, which fall at the lower end of the

Saxon range. This was also the case at Faccombe (Sadler 1990) and medieval Southampton (Bourdillon 1988), although not at Flaxengate (O'Connor 1982).

As in the Saxon assemblages, there are some quite small horse bones – for example, a pelvis from Lot's Hole with an acetabulum length (LAR) of 50.2 mm – and there is the possibility that they are in fact donkey. However, no specimens of donkey were identified in the cheek teeth or metapodials; other measurements, although typically indicating small animals, are within the range of contemporary southern British horses (Centre for Human Ecology 1995).

The relative proportions of the main domestic mammals at Lot's Hole and Lake End Road East are more similar in the medieval assemblages than they were in the Saxon, although it seems that pig may still have been more common and sheep and cattle less so at Lake End Road East. The relative importance of pig and sheep at these sites is the reverse of that evident at Jenning's Yard, Windsor (Bourdillon 1993). The larger numbers of sheep present at sites such as Jenning's Yard, Walton (Noddle 1976) and Aylesbury (Jones 1983) could have come from flocks kept on the chalk, where there may have been more suitable pasture for them and far less risk of footrot.

Grant (1988) has shown that rural medieval sites generally have a higher proportion of pig than do urban sites, and this can be seen at the manor of Faccombe (Sadler 1990); however the representation of sheep is still unusually low for a rural medieval site. Grant also suggested that high levels of pig and low levels of sheep could occur at high status sites. However, there is no other evidence from the animal bones at Lot's Hole and Lake End Road East to indicate particularly high status: one would also expect good representation of game animals at such sites, and although both red and roe deer occur at Lot's Hole the number of bones is very small. Environment is likely to have been an important influence, which would also account for the similarity between the Saxon and medieval assemblages: much of Buckinghamshire was still wooded at the time of the Domesday survey and raising pigs was an important activity (Trow-Smith 1957), and the manor of Dorney itself had pannage for 150 pigs (Morris 1978). The presence of the deer at Lot's Hole suggests the proximity of wooded areas.

The age of slaughter in the medieval assemblage is noticeably higher than that of the Saxon assemblage, suggesting more of a producer type economy in contrast to the consumer pattern of the Saxon material. Some animal breeding is suggested by the presence of the calf skeletons at Lake End Road East, but they could also have been casualties of disease rather than culling policy.

The contribution of domestic birds to the diet appears to have been minimal, although domestic fowl is always the most frequent species represented. In contrast to the Saxon period there is little evidence of wild-fowling: the pigeon bones from Lake End Road East may have been from wild or domestic birds although if the latter it suggests possible high status since dovecotes were a prerogative of the nobility. The presence of deer bones could support this interpretation: the frequency of deer bones actually increases from 0.6% in the Saxon to 2.5% in the medieval assemblage. However, this is still a very small proportion and hunted or possibly poached game would not have provided significant dietary input.

The role of the horse in the medieval period at Lot's Hole and Lake End Road East is worth comment. From studying demesne accounts Langdon (1982) argued that horses had a working life of five to seven years, depending on the nature of the work, while non-demesne animals would have had a less intensive workload in spite of more versatility being required of them. This would suggest that the latter had longer working lives, particularly if they had previously been demesne animals, resulting in an older archaeological age profile. However, only one or possibly two of the horses at Lot's Hole reflect this, while the others were probably still of working age. This could suggest that the horses here may have been worked hard under poor conditions, since there can be little reason to kill a horse unless it is worn out or has had a crippling accident.

The post-medieval period

A small quantity of animal bone was recovered from post-medieval material contexts, almost all from Lake End Road East; the material was not subjected to detailed analysis.

At Lake End Road East fragments of cattle are the most frequent and include a skull showing butchery marks and with the horn cores missing, possibly removed for horn working. The relatively numerous dog remains consist mostly of fragments (36) from one skull. Sheep and pig remains occur in similar numbers, with the pig bones including a male mandible pair and a mandible from a juvenile animal.

Horse is present in smaller numbers of which seven fragments comprise an articulating group of carpals and metacarpal. Rabbit (*Oryctolagus cuniculus*) and rat (*Rattus* sp.) are each represented by a single bone.

The post-medieval phase at Lot's Hole is represented by the largely complete skeleton (186 fragments) of an adult dog, found in the top fill (50816) of a post-medieval ditch.

The human bone
by Angela Boyle

A single neonate human bone was recovered from the fill (30425) of a pit (30426) at Lake End Road East. The pit was located within an area of post-medieval gravel quarrying. Pottery from the pit fill dates the feature to the mid 16th to the 17th century.

Long bone length has been used to estimate the likely age of the neonate from whom the bone came, using the regression formulae of Scheuer *et al.* (1980). This provided an estimate of 37.5385 ± 2.33 weeks. The bone has been identified as a right humerus. The bone must be redeposited from a grave, but no other evidence of burial was found on the site.

The charred plant remains
by Ruth Pelling

Six environmental samples were analysed in detail from medieval features at Lake End Road East and Lot's Hole. They provide evidence of grain use and processing and a variety of natural flora.

Lot's Hole

Seven samples were taken from deposits dating from the 10th to the 15th century. Most deposits produced low concentrations of cereal grains, occasional legumes, chaff and weeds with occasional charcoal flecks. The density of remains was in the region of 2–3 items per litre. In contrast the samples from two deposits (context 50661, pit 50480; context 51424, pit 51425) produced high concentrations of remains – in the case of context 50661, in excess of 1000 items per litre. The most common item in the remains was mostly identified as free-threshing *Triticum* sp. Legumes and weeds were also present.

Lake End Road East

Eighteen samples were taken from ten pits, including a cess pit. Three, with higher densities of remains were fully analysed (context 30520, pit 30519; context 30523, pit 30521; context 30449, pit 30448); a sample from a cess pit (30441) contained mineralised material which is characteristic of poorly drained deposits with a high faecal/urine content in conjunction with calcium carbonate (Green 1979). This deposit contained a range of fruit seeds, some deriving from locally grown fruit, others most likely from imported dried fruit.

Charred cereal remains

Charred remains were analysed from three pit deposits, contexts 30449 (pit 30448), 30520 (pit 30519) and 30523 (pit 30521), in which they were present in densities of 35 to 80 items per litre. Contexts 30523 and 30449 were dominated by weed seeds, forming 93% and 85.5% of the assemblages. Conversely cereal grains form the greatest component of context 30520 (56%). Weeds, chaff and legumes each form between 13% and 20%.

The Eton Rowing Course Project
by Mark Robinson

Only a few medieval deposits were available for analysis from Dorney. The pollen sequence from the Area 3 palaeochannel extended into the Saxon period, whereas the insect and macroscopic plant sequences from the same section probably only continued until the end of the Roman period. Alluvial sediments were, however, also sampled from above some Roman ditches in Area 20 and waterlogged organic sediment was sampled from the bottom of an early medieval pond in Area 6.

Methods and results

Mollusc remains from layer 11110 in the medieval pond (11111) were fragmentary and badly leached, and preservation of organic remains was poor but a useful quantity of macroscopic plant remains could be identified.

Floodplain vegetation

The molluscan assemblages from Samples 3210 and 3209 in Area 20 were characteristic of damp grassland. *Trichia hispida* gp. was most numerous but *Vallonia pulchella* was also present. The same species are numerous in hay meadow faunas on the floodplain of the Upper Thames Valley (Robinson 1988). Although shell concentrations were low in the samples from Area 20, a tentative interpretation of floodmeadow vegetation can be made from the results.

Flooding and alluviation

Riverine aquatic molluscs were absent from Samples 3210 and 3209, but they did contain shells of the amphibious snail *Lymnaea truncatula*, which in the upper Thames valley flourishes in pools of receding floodwater (Robinson 1988).

The most numerous seeds from Sample 2300, the medieval pond in Area 6, were of *Alisma* sp. (water plantain), a shallow water emergent or bankside plant likely to have been growing around the margin of the pond. Otherwise, the macroscopic plant remains suggest the floodplain to have been very open. There was a strong grassland element to the flora, with seeds of *Ranunculus* cf. *repens* (creeping buttercup) and *Prunella vulgaris* (selfheal). Seeds were also present of two species favoured by hay meadow conditions: *Rhinanthus* sp. (hay meadow) and *Leucanthemum vulgare* (ox-eye daisy).

Conclusions

The results from the alluvium in Area 20 and pond 11111 in Area 6 both suggest at least some of the floodplain at Dorney to have been seasonally flooded hay meadow during the medieval period. The height at which alluvium was being deposited in Area 20 was greater than earlier alluviation. There results are very similar to the picture given by the environmental evidence from the Upper Thames Valley (Robinson 1992).

Chapter 8:   Discussion of the Medieval and Post-Medieval Archaeology

by John Hiller, Alan Hardy and Tim Allen

At both Lot's Hole and Lake End Road East, the medieval and post-medieval deposits were accorded a lower priority than the middle Saxon material in the excavation programme and the post-excavation research programmes, so less detailed conclusions can be drawn (see Chapters 1 & 2). The medieval and post-medieval development of the sites is considered in turn, along with their significance within a regional context.

LOT'S HOLE (INCLUDING THE GRAVEL STORAGE AREA)

In broad terms, the evidence recovered from the site points to a fairly modest settlement in existence for 150 years or more from the second half of the 11th century to sometime in the first half of the 13th century. The start date of occupation is suggested by the presence of five fairly common Saxo-Norman pottery fabrics, and for the end date the absence of medieval 'established' wares dating to the late 13th–15th centuries which occur at Lake End Road East. After the settlement was abandoned the evidence suggests that the landscape of the settled area was incorporated into the existing layout of rectangular fields, some of the boundaries of which are echoed in the 1812 estate map (see Fig. 1.7) and modern air photographs (see Pl. 1.1).

The nature of the evidence lends itself to being considered in two stages – the arrangement and evolution of the sequence of enclosures, and the buildings – their construction, disposition, function and relation to the enclosures.

The enclosures and their development

There is no evidence of direct continuity between the middle Saxon activity, which appears to have ended in the second half of the 8th century, and the late Saxon activity which appears to have begun no earlier than the 11th century. However, both the droveway and the interrupted ditch of Phase 2, oriented NE-SW, could be leading to one of the middle Saxon trackways running north-east through the Lake End Road West site – quite possibly the one identified as a legacy of the Roman farmstead. Interestingly, there is no indication that either the ditch or droveway respects the edge of the palaeochannel alongside the west of the site. The presence of Saxo-Norman pottery in the ditch fills indicates occupation, but only one building (51993) was located alongside the ditch, and no obvious focus of occupation is evident.

The establishment and development of the settlement in the 12th and early 13th centuries is dominated by the large curved enclosure, which seems to have been established in open ground, not part of any larger field system. Initially a possible water hole was the only feature present within the enclosure, the buildings and associated rubbish pits being outside. It is suggested that this represents a stock enclosure belonging to a single farm. However, the size of the enclosure (even in its first phase), and its relation to the palaeochannel is somewhat untypical of medieval rural farmsteads.

Examination of medieval rural settlements – for instance Westbury in Buckinghamshire (Ivens *et al.* 1995, fig. 73) – tend to point to an organic growth of settlement, with clusters of buildings and relatively modest rectangular fields or paddocks. At Lot's Hole we could be looking at the establishment of specialised enterprise rather than an evolving farm complex.

By the later 12th century, the enclosure was enlarged, but still essentially the dominant feature of the settlement. Some buildings are now within the enclosure, some apparently still outside. Those outside are aligned with linear features extending to the north-east, suggesting that the enclosure is by now incorporated into a larger rectilinear land division, although its function has not necessarily altered.

By the late 14th century the curved enclosure was abandoned, and the area fully incorporated into the rectilinear field system. The close association of the enclosure with the buildings immediately inside and outside is emphasised by the fact that they are abandoned too. Two buildings (51826 and 50193) identified during the excavation possibly belong to this final phase, and with them maybe Building X in the Gravel Storage Area. The overall division of the landscape thereafter persisted through into the post-medieval period.

The buildings *(Figs 6.3–5 & Table 8.1)*

Thirteen distinct buildings or structures were identified, all represented by arrangements of negative features – postholes and/or beam slots. In no case was this evidence supplemented by surviving floor layers or coherent hearth surfaces. One of the buildings (51993) possibly pre-dated the curved

Table 8.1   Lot's Hole buildings

Structure	Type	Dim (m)	Or	%c	RP	IP	D	H	Da	EB	Pits	Phase
51993	PH	c 15 × 5	W-E	70	2	?	N	N	Y	Y	N	2
51452	PH	7.0 × 3.0	N-S	60	–	–	N	N	N	Y	Y	3
51880	PH/BS	8.0 × 6.0	W-E	60	2	3	Y	N	N	N	Y	3
52002	PH	4.7 × 3.5	N-S	80?	–	–	N	N	N	N	N	4
51567	PH	7.0 × 5.5	N-S	80	2	–	N	N	Y	N	N	4
51270	PH	10.5 × 4.5	N-S	100	–	–	Y	N	N	N	N	4
51881	PH/BS	14.5 × 9.0	W-E	80	2	2	Y	Y	Y	N	Y	4
50664	PH/BS	12.0 × 8.5	W-E	60	–	2	Y	N	Y	N	Y	4
51597	PH	10.0 × 5.0	W-E	80	–	3	N	N	Y	N	Y	4
52001	PH	c11.0 × 5.0	W-E	100	–	–	?	N	Y	N	Y	4
51826	PH	9.0 × 6.3	W-E	100	–	3	N	N	N	N	N	5
50193	BS?	4.9 dia	–	100	–	–	–	–	–	–	N	5
Building X	PH	10.0 × 6.0	W-E	100	?3	–	N	N	N	N	Y	5

PH – Earthfast post construction
BS – Beam slot construction
Dim – Dimensions in plan
Or – Orientation (approximate)
%c – Footprint – percentage complete
RP – Ridge postholes
IP – Other internal postholes
D – Doorway identified
H – Hearth identified
Da – Presence of daub within footprint or associated features
EB – ?External bracing
Pits – Nearby pits?
Ph – Interpreted phase

enclosure, and three (Building X, 51826, and 50193) have been assigned to Phase 5, post-dating the enclosure. The nine buildings/structures associated with the two phases of enclosure display some common features in their construction.

Building construction

Seven of the nine buildings related to the enclosure were constructed using spaced individual postholes. The spacing varied, both between buildings and within individual walls. In only one building (50664) were the postholes spaced with clear regularity, although the temptation to attribute higher status to the building because of this fact alone should be resisted.

A number of buildings displayed similar characteristics of construction, suggesting a certain uniformity in the building style, and arguably implying continuity of the community. Two of the buildings (51880 and 51881) displayed internal postholes in opposing corners, possibly representing purlin supports, or some form of internal partition or furniture. Both of these buildings also had evidence of sill beam slots as well as discrete postholes, in addition to ridge postholes.

In some cases fragments of daub were found associated with each building, probably remnants of wall covering, which presumably was plastered over a wattle screen fixed between (or possibly over) the post uprights.

Building function

The structural evidence alone cannot indicate the buildings' function with any clarity. Many of the buildings can be equally well explained as houses, or as agricultural outbuildings such as barns or byres. This does not in itself mean that the buildings were of low standard, merely that timber-framed construction was adaptable for many uses – the surviving elements of a ground plan do not in themselves necessarily provide a clear diagnostic basis.

A few functional distinctions can be inferred, however. The two buildings with vestigial remains of hearths can reasonably be assumed to have been dwellings. Those buildings with nearby pits can also be assumed to have accommodated people. The buildings with no hearth or nearby pits were quite probably animal shelters. One building (51597) – clearly associated with the second phase of the enclosure, but set well apart from the others – may have been a store for grain or straw.

In the context of the interpretation of the enclosure and its function, it may be significant that none of the buildings associated with the enclosure displayed any evidence of an interior partition wall, often associated with the 'longhouse' where animals

and humans shared accommodation (The only building with such a partition wall was Building X, in Phase 5 – see below). This characteristic may reinforce the idea that this was an organised settlement with a single function, rather than a group of independent single family units.

The buildings of Phase 5

Two of the three buildings associated with Phase 5 show clear differences to those of Phases 3 and 4.

The semicircular structure (50193)

This was situated close to the western edge of the site, and represented by a semicircular slot. The vertically-sided and flat-bottomed slot is presumed to have housed a timber beam foundation, although such a presumption is based purely on its similarity to straight beam slots, and cannot be demonstrated. As to the character or function of any superstructure, there are few clues. The structure is sited some distance from any other building, which could suggest a utilitarian function, possible a hay rick or grain store.

Building X

Given that none of the elements of this building were excavated, little can be deduced from the plan except that the presence of an internal partition wall suggests that this may represent a more typical small agricultural dwelling than those of Phases 3 and 4. Examples of these two-cell houses are many; built in stone or timber, they represent the basic small farmstead dwelling of the medieval period. Traces of a two-cell timber house of the 12th century were recently excavated at Northfleet Kent (Hardy and Bell 2001). Recent examples dating to the 13th century have been excavated at Fringford, Oxfordshire (Blinkhorn *et al.* 2000) and Old Grimsbury, Oxfordshire (Hardy 2000).

The settlement character and function

The close association evident between the buildings and the large enclosure suggests a common or related function. The artefactual evidence recovered does not provide many clues. The pottery is unremarkable and consistently lacking in wares suggestive of status or routine connection with regional centres (like Windsor). Similarly, the few notable and diagnostic pieces among the metalwork assemblage appear to post-date the enclosure. The animal bone assemblage broadly reflects an expected predominance of the three main domestic species, cattle, sheep and pigs, with a slight emphasis on the latter, possibly due to the likely proximity of at least intermittent woodland. It may be significant, however, that Powell does highlight the presence of horses and deer, in higher numbers than might be expected in a settlement of apparently low status.

Powell suggests that the horses were of a mature age, and showed signs of a hard life and eventual butchery – possibly not what one would expect if horse-breeding were taking place. However, if horse breeding were practised here, would it necessarily show in the animal bone assemblage? The specimens found need not have been part of the breeding stock. It is also true that the deer can be explained as the spoils of poaching, but this is only one possibility.

It is perhaps significant that the documentary history examined in Chapter 1 notes the record of 'horse pasture' at Dorney in the Domesday survey. In the context of the later reference to the establishment of a stud farm at 'Le Parke' in the 14th century, one may postulate a local tradition of horse breeding, exploiting the local meadow grasses, which are especially important in this context (Gladitz 1997, 151). It is therefore possible that at Lot's Hole we have evidence of a secondary settlement, perhaps a dependency of the manor at Dorney, established specifically for the breeding of horses and centred on the organised exploitation of the well-watered meadow grasses north of the manor. There appear to have been three types of building; the dwelling, usually based upon a timber frame sill-beam constructed hall (51880, 51881); the barn, or animal shelter (51270, 51567) based upon earthfast post construction, lacking internal ridge or aisle posts, and agricultural buildings (grain or fodder stores?) like 51597. The settlement focus appears to have been accessed from the north-east, from a track leading off a north-south road leading from Dorney west of (and possibly a forerunner to) Lake End Road itself.

The late medieval and post-medieval periods

No evidence was found for any significant activity in the late medieval period or post-medieval period. From the later map evidence (Pls 1.2–3) the major field boundaries appear to survive, but artefactual evidence is restricted to a few post-medieval coins recovered from the excavated topsoil.

LAKE END ROAD EAST

The medieval occupation

The chronology of the medieval occupation evidence at Lake End Road East is difficult to refine beyond the broad start and finish dates. The limited number of features excavated, coupled with the evident degree of redeposition in the finds assemblages, means that resort must be made to the limited stratigraphic evidence and possible spatial relationships.

If one trend is apparent, however, it is that the medieval enclosures seem to display a consistency of shape, size and orientation which suggests a continuity in the nature of the settlement of which they are a part. It seems likely that they would have been related to properties fronting the road.

Although the modern road edge was immediately adjacent to the western edge of the site, the original lane would presumably have been considerably narrower.

Only one probable structure was revealed, in the form of the posthole cluster in the south-west corner of the site. In the absence of hard dating evidence, it seems likely that this building was an outbuilding associated with a roadside dwelling.

Economy and status

A few details from the evidence recovered allow some tentative conclusions to be drawn. The preponderance of pig bones in proportion to sheep and cattle may point to the mainstay occupation of the inhabitants in the medieval period, although we have no way of knowing how large the individual properties were. These paddocks, close to the road and the house, may have been specifically for pigs, or possibly young animals (there is some evidence in the bone assemblage for the presence of calves). There is no suggestion of enhanced status in the settlement until the later medieval period, when a few items suggest that at least one nearby property of some sophistication has been constructed. The roof finial (see Chapter 7), and the flint-lined pits suggest a building of some quality nearby, and the presence of a number of 'established' wares within the late medieval pottery assemblage (which is in contrast to their near complete absence from the medieval site at Lot's Hole) suggest more contact with regional centres. A slight hint of a more exotic diet could be read into the presence of bones of young pigeons (squabs), which could have derived from a dovecote. However, dovecotes were usually only the preserve of wealthy and high status individuals – certainly significantly higher than the apparent status of the medieval inhabitants along Lake End Road.

A key factor in the establishment and development of settlement alongside the road may have been the establishment of Burnham Abbey in 1266 to the north. The road between Burnham and Dorney would have become the main north-south route in the vicinity, supplanting the trackways that possibly survived from the Saxon period. The formal establishment of the manor house in Dorney in *c* 1500 could well have given further impetus to the status of the immediate area.

The post-medieval period

In the post-medieval period the focus of activity appeared to be more restricted to the quarry area and its immediate surroundings. This may imply that property division or ownership along the road had changed, or properties had been amalgamated. Neither Rocque's map of 1761 (Pl. 2.1) nor the 1812 Estate map (Pl. 2.2) show any buildings along the eastern side of the road at this point, although the wells, and the small assemblage of architectural fragments (see CD-ROM) again hint at buildings of at least some sophistication nearby.

THE MEDIEVAL SETTLEMENTS AT LOT'S HOLE AND LAKE END ROAD EAST IN THEIR REGIONAL CONTEXT

Current research into the nature and development of medieval rural settlement has greatly enhanced the understanding of regional patterns and idiosyncrasies. In their study of medieval settlement within the four counties of Buckinghamshire, Bedfordshire, Northamptonshire and Leicestershire, Lewis *et al*. (2001) have noted a striking absence of nucleated villages in the area between the Thames and the Chilterns. Instead, and attested by historical as well as archaeological evidence, there are 'dispersed settlements' – loose (though not necessarily any more temporary) agglomerations of houses and paddocks. Such settlements are perhaps best defined by what they are not, and what they do not have; they typically have no church or manor house as a focus (although they may belong to a manor). Many are sited close to parish boundaries or established villages, and may represent secondary settlements; their buildings may straggle along a road or track, but not always one that survives beyond the lifetime of the settlement (ibid. 113). Unlike nucleated settlements, they often do not have a surrounding and established field system.

From the Domesday survey, the population density of the area immediately north of the Thames at this point was significantly low, no more than seven per square mile (ibid. 136), probably less than half the population density of river valleys further north.

The very nature of dispersed settlements makes their identification by archaeological or landscape evidence difficult, with no clear arrangement of tofts or dense pottery scatters to signal a clear presence. Systematic fieldwalking surveys, such as took place in Northamptonshire in the 1970s, can register many small settlements, but confirmatory programmes of excavation are rarely achievable on a scale large enough to draw firm conclusions about the density (ibid. 15).

Conclusion

On the basis of the evidence from this project, the settlement at Lot's Hole seems to fit best in the category of a secondary dispersed settlement. Its unusual layout however, with its suggestion of a specialised function, sets it apart and does not allow easy comparisons. The evidence at Lake End Road East is less distinctive, but could also represent secondary settlement along the road between Dorney and Burnham.

It is the safe assumption to say that both settlements were economically tied to the closest manors, but the characteristics of Lot's Hole in particular might suggest that its livestock produce was destined for further afield – possibly London.

THE ETON ROWING COURSE PROJECT
by Tim Allen

Although the medieval evidence from the Eton Rowing Course is very limited, it has provided useful support for the suggestion, based upon post-medieval map evidence, that the silted palaeochannels of the Thames were used throughout the medieval period as hay meadows (see Chapter 2, Historical background). Both the water hole close to the Cress Brook channel and the molluscs from alluvium in Area 20 suggest medieval hay meadows close by. Taken in conjunction with the likely late medieval ditch crossing Area 20, it suggests that not only the Cress Brook but also Channel N were used for hay in late medieval times. Continued use as hay meadows may also explain the small but mixed concentration of late medieval and post-medieval pottery found on the palaeochannel edge in Area 3, the result not of manuring scatters but of vessels brought and broken by locals during hay-making.

Chapter 9:   Conclusion

by Alan Hardy

The archaeological evidence considered in this volume shows a landscape retaining a pattern of agricultural exploitation of the pasture, hay meadows and light woodland which seems to have evolved from the Roman period or earlier. However, for reasons that even fieldwork on the scale of these two projects cannot clearly define, the landscape seems to have lent itself to temporary occupation, rather than sustained and developing settlement.

The Roman settlement is abandoned well before the end of the 4th century. After this period there is little evidence for permanent occupation, although there is no clear evidence that the character of the landscape radically changed. Traces of early Saxon activity are ephemeral, in the form of residual emmer wheat and pottery at Lake End Road and the isolated burial at Area 6 (Eton Rowing Course).

The middle Saxon pits found at Lake End Road West and Lot's Hole represent an unusual site and one that is difficult to parallel. Our suggested interpretation is that it represents a form of temporary gathering, perhaps short-lived, of some status and perhaps involving hundreds of people. Why did these people gather at this place, on what was a relatively flat and characterless piece of land? There are no known settlements within the immediate area, while recorded Saxon activity within the area of the Eton Rowing Course and in the area bounded by the Flood Alleviation Scheme is evidently scarce. It is accepted that it is still possible that any contemporary settlement is masked by later settlement, although to date there is no evidence to support this suggestion.

Maybe the very anonymity of the place was its attraction. Further upriver is the possible power centre at Taplow, with its high status burial and reuse of an Iron Age hillfort, and later establishment of a church within the defences, and downriver is the town and royal palace site of Old Windsor.

Whatever the purpose of the middle Saxon gathering it appears to have had little or no lasting impact on the landscape, and there is no indication that the medieval settlements owe their disposition or character to the event.

If the motivation of the middle Saxon gathering remains unknown, there are aspects to the evidence of the medieval settlement which might represent specialised exploitation of the landscape. Such specialisation may have been encouraged by the relatively unpopulated and undeveloped nature of this area. By this time, centres of settlement like Taplow and Windsor had developed, leaving the area around Dorney and Boveney as a relatively unpopulated backwater in a bend of the river, valuable agricultural land held by a number of different manors. Such settlement as did accumulate tended to be of a dispersed and (as in the case of the medieval settlement at Lot's Hole) sometimes transitory nature.

It can be suggested that the area studied is a landscape where, by a combination of its resources, topography and the nature of surrounding territory, the circumstances have mitigated against a permanent developing settlement of any size. Without the magnet of such a settlement, activities which did take place have been relatively ephemeral and as such have left little of an easily recognised identity in the archaeological record. It follows that archaeological evidence that is found in such an area, as in the case of the middle Saxon pits, may be of special, and possibly unique, character.

Bibliography

Addyman, P V, 1964 A Dark Age Settlement at Maxey, Northants, *Medieval Archaeol* **8**, 20–73

Ager, B, 1989 The Anglo-Saxon cemetery, in *Verulamium; The King Harry Lane site* (I M Stead and V Rigby), 219–39, English Heritage Archaeol Rep, London

Albarella, U and Davis, S J M, forthcoming The Saxon and Medieval Animal Bone, in Chapman forthcoming

Allen, T G and Lamdin-Whymark H, 2000 The rediscovery of Taplow Hillfort, *South Midlands Archaeol* (CBA South Midlands Grp) **30**, 22–8

Allen, T G and Lamdin-Whymark H, 2001 The Taplow Hillfort, *Curr Archaeol* **175**, 286–9

Allen, T G and Welsh, K, 1996 Eton Rowing Lake, Dorney, Buckinghamshire, *South Midlands Archaeol* (CBA South Midlands Grp) **26**, 23–30

Andrews, P (ed.), 1997 *Excavations at Hamwic*: 2, CBA Res Rep **109**

Andrews, P and Metcalf, M, 1997 The coins, in Andrews 1997, 210–15

Anon, 1970 Roman Britain in 1969, *Britannia* **1**, 301–2

Anon, 1971 Roman Britain in 1970, *Britannia* **2**, 284

Anon, 1972 Roman Britain in 1971, *Britannia* **3**, 349–50

Arkell, W J, 1939 A map of the Corallian Beds between Marcham and Faringdon, Berkshire, *Proc Geol Ass* **50**, 487–509

Astill, G G and Lobb S J, 1989 Excavations of Prehistoric, Roman and Saxon Deposits at Wraysbury, Berkshire, *Archaeol J* **146**, 68–134

Bailey, K, 1989 The Middle Saxons, in *The origin of Anglo-Saxon Kingdoms* (ed. S Bassett), 108–22, Leicester

Bennett, C M, 1962 Cox Green Roman Villa, *Berkshire Archaeol J* **60**, 62–92

Biddle, M, 1973 Winchester, the development of an early capital, *Vor- und Frühformen der europaischen Stadt im Mittelalter* **235**, 242–3, Göttingen

Blackmore, L, 1988 The Anglo-Saxon pottery, in two Middle Saxon occupation sites: excavations at Jubilee Hall and 21–22 Maiden Lane (R L Whytehead and R Cowie with L Blackmore), *Trans London Middlesex Archaeol Soc* **39**, 81–110

Blackmore, L, 1997 From Beach to burh: new clues to entity and identity in 7th- to 9th-century London, in *Urbanism in medieval Europe–Papers of the medieval Brugge 1997 conference* **1** (eds Guy de Boe and F Verhaeghe), 123–32, Zellik

Blair, J, 1989 Friuthwold's Kingdom and the Origins of Surrey, in *The origins of Anglo-Saxon kingdoms* (ed S Bassett), 97–107, Leicester

Blair, W J, 1994 *Anglo-Saxon Oxfordshire,* Stroud

Blair, W J, 1996 The Minsters of the Thames, in *The cloister and the world: essays in medieval history in honour of Barbara Harvey* (eds J Blair and B Golding), 5–28, Oxford

Blinkhorn, P W, 1994 Early Saxon pottery, in *Bancroft, a late Bronze Age settlement, Roman villa and temple mausoleum* (R J Williams and R J Zeepvat), Buckinghamshire Archaeol Soc Monog Ser **7**, 512–4

Blinkhorn, P W, 1999 Of cabbages and kings: production, trade and the rural economy in middle Saxon England, in *Beyond the Emporia* (ed M J Anderton), 4–23, Sheffield University

Blinkhorn, P W, forthcoming The post-Roman pottery, in *Excavations at North Raunds, Northamptonshire* (M Audouy), English Heritage Monog Ser

Blockley, K, Blockley, M, Blockley, P, Frere, S S and Stow, S, 1995 Excavations in the Marlowe car park and surrounding areas, *The archaeology of Canterbury* **5**, Whitstable

Bourdillon, J, 1988 Countryside and town: the animal resources of Saxon Southampton, in *Anglo-Saxon settlements* (ed. D Hooke), 177–95, Oxford

Bourdillon, J, 1993 Animal bone, in *Jennings Yard, Windsor: a closed-shaft garderobe and associated medieval structures* (eds J W Hawkes and M J Heaton), Wessex Archaeol Rep **3**, 67–79, Salisbury

Bourdillon, J with Andrews, P, 1997 The animal bone, in *Excavations at Hamwic*, **2** (ed P Andrews), CBA Res Rep **109**, 242–5, York

Boyle, A, Jennings, D, Miles, D and Palmer, S, 1998 *The Anglo-Saxon cemetery at Butler's Field, Lechlade, Gloucestershire. Volume 1: prehistoric and Roman activity and grave catalogue*, Thames Valley Landscapes Monogr **10**, Oxford

Brodribb, A C C, Hands, A R and Walker, D R, 1972 *Excavations at Shakenoak Farm, near Wilcote, Oxfordshire. Part III: Site F,* privately published

Brooks, N, 1971 The development of military obligation in 8th and 9th century England, in *England before the Conquest* (eds P Clemoes and K Hughes), 69–84, Oxford

Brown, P D C, 1972 The iron objects, in A C Brodribb *et al.* 1972, 86–117

Brown, P D C, 1977 The significance of the Londesborough ring brooch, *Antiq J* **57**, 95–7

Brown, T J, 1969 *The Durham Ritual, a southern English collectar of the tenth century, with Northumbrian additions* Durham Cathedral Library A.IV.**19**, 24, Copenhagen

Campbell, E M J, 1971 Buckinghamshire, in *The Domesday geography of south-east England* (eds H C Darby and E M J Campbell), 138–86, London

Canham, R, 1979 Excavations at Shepperton Green, 1967 and 1973, *Trans London Middlesex Archaeol Soc* **30**, 97–124

Carstairs, P, 1986a The Dorney Study: an archaeological implications report, unpublished report, Buckinghamshire County Museum

Carstairs, P, 1986b An archaeological study of the Dorney area, *Rec Buckinghamshire* **28**, 163–8

Centre for Human Ecology, 1995 *Animal Bone Metrical Archive Project (ABMAP). Draft Report on the Project Phase for English Heritage*, Centre for Human Ecology, Department of Archaeology, University of Southampton

Chapman, A, forthcoming *West Cotton: a study in settlement dynamics. Excavations at West Cotton, Raunds, Northamptonshire, 1985–1989*, English Heritage Monogr Ser

Chenevix-Trench, J, 1973 Coleshill and the Settlements of the Chilterns, *Rec Buckinghamshire* **19**, 241–58

Clark, J, 1995 *The Medieval horse and its equipment*, Medieval finds from excavations in London **5**, Museum of London, London

Cowie, R and Whytehead, R L, 1988 Two Middle Saxon occupation sites: excavations at Jubilee Hall and 21–22 Maiden Lane, *Trans London Middlesex Archaeol Soc* **39**, 47–163

Coy, J P, 1980 The animal bones, in Excavation of a mid-Saxon iron smelting site at Ramsbury, Wiltshire (ed. J Haslam), *Medieval Archaeol* **24**, 41–51

Coy, J P, 1989 Animal bones, in Astill, G G, and Lobb, S J, 1989, 11–124

Crabtree, P J, 1996 Production and consumption in an early complex society: animal use in Middle Saxon East Anglia, *World Archaeol* **28**, 58–75

Cram, L, 1986–1990 Faunal remains, in Excavations and observations of Bronze Age and Saxon deposits at Brimpton, 1978–1979 (S Lobb), *Berkshire Archaeol J* **73**, 51–3

Cramp, R J, Everson, P and Hall, D N, 1977 Excavations at Brixworth 1971 and 1972, *J Brit Archaeol Ass* **130**, 52–132

Cubitt, C, 1995 *Anglo-Saxon Church Councils, c. 680-c. 850*, Leicester

Dickinson, T M, 1976 The Anglo-Saxon burial sites of the Upper Thames region, and their bearing on the history of Wessex, *c.* AD 400–700, unpubl. DPhil thesis, Univ Oxford

Drewett P, Rudling, D, and Gardiner, M, 1988 *A regional history of England: the south-east to AD 1000*, 287–341, London and New York

Dunning, G C, Hurst, J G, Myres, J N L, and Tischler, F, 1959 Anglo-Saxon pottery: a symposium, *Medieval Archaeol* **3**, 1–78

Egan, G, and Pritchard, F, 1991 *Dress accessories c. 1150–1450. Medieval finds from excavations in London (3)*, HMSO, London

Evison, V I, 1987 *Dover: the Buckland Anglo-Saxon cemetery*, HBMC Archaeol Rep **3**, London

Farley, M, 1976 Saxon and medieval Walton, Aylesbury: excavations 1973–1974, *Rec Buckinghamshire* **20**, 153–290

Faussett, B, 1856 *Inventorium Sepulchrale*, (ed. C Roach Smith), London

Fisher, G C, 1979 Finger rings of the early Saxon period, unpublished MPhil thesis, Univ Oxford

Ford, S, 1986 A newly discovered causewayed enclosure at Eton Wick, near Windsor, Berks, *Proc Prehist Soc* **52**, 319–20

Ford, S, 1987 *East Berkshire Survey*, Berkshire Department of Highways and Planning, Occas Pap **1**

Ford, S, 1991 Maidenhead, Windsor and Eton Flood Alleviation Scheme archaeological evaluation stage 3, Thames Valley Archaeol Services unpublished evaluation report

Ford, S, 1998 Excavation of middle Iron Age and early Roman enclosures and field systems, an early/middle Bronze Age cremation cemetery, and Neolithic and middle Bronze Age deposits, at Cippenham Sector, Wood Lane extension, Slough, Berkshire, Thames Valley Archaeological Services archive report for Eton College

Gates, T, 1975 *The Middle Thames Valley: an archaeological survey of the river gravels*, Berkshire Archaeol Comm Publ **1**, [Reading]

Gladitz, C, 1997 *Horse breeding in the medieval world*, Dublin

Grant, A, 1988 Animal resources, in *The countryside of medieval England* (eds G Astill and A Grant), 149–87, Oxford

Green, F J, 1979 Phosphate mineralisation of seeds from archaeological sites, *J Archaeol Sci* **6.3**, 279–84

Griffiths, N, 1986 *Horse harness pendants*, Finds Research Group 700–1700, Datasheet 5, Coventry

Griffiths, N, 1989 *Shield-shaped mounts*, Finds Research Group 700–1700, Datasheet 12, Oxford

Griffiths, N, 1995 Horse pendants and associated fittings, in Clark 1995, 61–71

Hagen, A, 1995 *A handbook of Anglo-Saxon food. Production and distribution*, Middlesex

Hall, D, 1982 *Medieval fields*, Princes Risborough

Hamerow, H, 1993 *Excavations at Mucking, vol. 2: the Anglo-Saxon settlement*, English Heritage, Archaeol Rep **21**, London

Hamerow, H, 1998 Angles, Saxons and Anglo-Saxons: rural centres, trade and production, in *Studien zur Sachsenforschung*, **13**, 189–205

Hamerow, H, 1999 Anglo-Saxon Oxfordshire, 400–700, *Oxoniensia* **64**, 23–32

Hardy, A, 2000 The excavation of a medieval cottage and associated agricultural features at Manor Farm Old Grimsbury, Banbury, *Oxoniensia* **65**, 345–80

Hardy, A and Bell, C, 2001 *The excavation of a medieval rural settlement at the Pepper Hill Lane electricity substation, Northfleet, Kent*, Oxford Archaeol Occas Pap **10**, Oxford

Hardy, A, Dodd, A and Keevill, G, forthcoming *Aelfric's Abbey: excavations at Eynsham Abbey, Oxfordshire 1989–1992* Oxford Archaeology, Thames Valley Monogr Ser

Haslam, J, 1980 A Middle Saxon iron smelting site at Ramsbury, Wiltshire, *Medieval Archaeol*, **79**, 1–68

Haslam, J, 1987 Market and fortress in the times of Offa, *World Archaeol* **19**, 76–93

Hawkes, S C and Grove, L R A, 1963 Finds from a seventh century Anglo-Saxon cemetery at Milton Regis, *Archaeol Cantiana* **78**, 22–38

Hawkes, S C, Merrick, J M and Metcalf, D M, 1966 X-ray fluorescent analysis of some Dark Age coins and jewellery, *Archaeometry* **9**, 98–147

Hedges, J D and Buckley, D G, 1985 Anglo-Saxon burials and later features excavated at Orsett, Essex 1975 *Medieval Archaeol* **29**, 1–24

Higham, N, 1990 Settlement, land use and Domesday ploughlands in the landscape, *Landscape Hist* **12**, 33–44

Hill, D, 1981, *An atlas of Anglo-Saxon England*, Oxford

Hill, J D, 1995 *Ritual and rubbish in the Iron Age of Wessex* BAR Brit Ser **242**, Oxford

HMSO 1875 *Return of the owners of land*, Vol. 1, London

Holden, E W, 1976 Excavations at Old Erringham, Shoreham, West Sussex; Part 1. A Saxon weaving hut, *Sussex Archaeol Collect* **114**, 306–21

Holdsworth, P, 1980 *Excavations at Melbourne Street, Southampton 1971–1976*, 79–121, CBA Res Rep **33**, London

Hunn, A, Lawson, J and Farley, M, 1990 Maidenhead, Windsor and Eton Flood Alleviation Scheme: a study of the archaeological implications, Buckinghamshire County Museum for National Rivers Authority (Thames Region), Reports I–III, unpublished

Hunn, J R, 1997 A report on the landscape history of the area along the Thames Flood Alleviation Channel between Maidenhead and Windsor, Archaeological Services and Consultancy Ltd, unpublished

Hunter J, 1980, The glass, in Holdsworth 1980, 59–72

Hurst, D. (ed.) 1983. *Bedae Venerabilis opera Pars 2: Opera exegetica*, Turnhout

Hurst, J G, 1959 Middle-Saxon pottery, in Anglo-Saxon pottery: a symposium (G C Dunning, J G Hurst, J N L Myers and F Tischler), *Medieval Archaeol* **3**, 13–31

Hyslop, M, 1963 Two Anglo-Saxon cemeteries at Chamberlain's Barn, Leighton Buzzard, Beds, *Archaeol J* **120**, 161–200

Ivens, R, Bushby, P and Shepherd, N, 1995 *Tattenhoe and Westbury: Two deserted medieval settlements in Milton Keynes*, Buckinghamshire Archaeol Soc. Monogr Ser **8**, Aylesbury

Jarvis, M G, Allen, R H, Fordham, S J, Hazelden, J, Moffat, A J and Sturdy, R G, 1984 Soils and their use in south-east England, *Soil Survey of England and Wales*, Bulletin **15**, Harpenden

Jones, G G, 1983 The medieval animal bones, in Iron Age occupation, a Middle Saxon cemetery, and twelfth to nineteenth century urban occupation: excavations in George Street, Aylesbury, 1981 (D Allen and C H Dalwood), *Rec Buckinghamshire* **25**, 31–44

Jones, P, 1984 Saxon and medieval pottery, in *Excavations at Staines 1975–1976: The Friends'-Burial Ground site* (K R Crouch and S A Shanks), joint publication London Middlesex Archaeol Soc and Surrey Archaeol Soc **2**, 74–9, [London]

Jones, P and Moorhouse, S, 1981 The Saxon and medieval pottery, in A group of Saxon and medieval finds from the site of a Neolithic causewayed enclosure at Staines, Surrey, with a note on the topography of the area (R Robertson-Mackay *et al.*), *Trans London Middlesex Archaeol Soc* **32**, 119–23

Kars, H, 1980 Early medieval Dorestad, an archaeological-petrological study, I: general introduction – the Tephrite querns, *Berichten van de Rijkdienst voor het Oudheidkundig Bodemonderzoek* **30**, 393–422

Kars, H, 1983 Early medieval Dorestad, an archaeological-petrological study. Part V: the whetstones and the touchstones, *Berichten van de Rijkdienst voor het Oudheidkundig Bodemonderzoek* **33**, 1–37

Lambrick, G, 1992 Alluvial archaeology of the Holocene in the Upper Thames basin 1971–1991: a review, in *Alluvial Archaeology in Britain* (eds S Needham and M G Macklin), Oxbow Monogr **27**, 209–26, Oxford

Langdon, J, 1982 The economics of horses and oxen in medieval England, *The Agricultural Hist Rev* **30**, 31–40

Leadam, I S (ed.), 1897 *Domesday of Enclosures 1517–18*, Roy Hist Soc, London

Leeds, E T and Harden, D B, 1936 *The Anglo-Saxon cemetery at Abingdon*, Oxford

Lewis, C, Mitchell-Fox, P and Dyer, C, 2001 *Village hamlet and field*, Macclesfield

MacGregor, A, 1982 *Anglo-Scandinavian finds from Lloyds Bank, Pavement and other sites*, The Archaeology of York **17/3**, London

MacGregor, A, Mainman, A J and Rogers, N S H, 1999 *Craft, industry and everyday life: bone, antler, ivory and horn from Anglo-Scandinavian and medieval York*, The Archaeology of York **17/12**, London

Mainman, A J and Rogers, N S H, 2000 *Craft, industry and everyday life: finds from Anglo-Scandinavian York*, The Archaeology of York **17/14**, York

Margeson, S, 1993 *Norwich households: the medieval and post-medieval finds from Norwich Survey excavations 1971–1978*, EAA **58**, Norwich

Mellor, M, 1994 Oxfordshire pottery: a synthesis of middle and late Saxon pottery and early post-medieval pottery in the Oxford Region, *Oxoniensia* **49**, 100–6

Morris, J, 1978 *Domesday Book: Buckinghamshire*, Chichester

Myres, J N L, 1977 *A corpus of Anglo-Saxon pottery of the pagan period*, Cambridge

Noddle, B, 1976 Report on the animal bone from Walton, in Saxon and medieval Walton, Aylesbury: excavations 1973–1974 (M Farley), *Rec Buckinghamshire* **20**, 269–89

Noël Hume, I, 1991 *A guide to the artefacts of colonial America*, (1969, reprinted), New York

OAU 1996 Old Windsor, proposed sewer and land drainage works, Archaeological desk-based assessment, unpublished

OAU 1997 Maidenhead, Windsor and Eton Flood Alleviation Scheme. Post-excavation assessment and updated project design, unpublished document prepared for the Environment Agency

OAU 1998 Maidenhead, Windsor and Eton Flood Alleviation Scheme Tranche 2. Post-excavation assessment and updated project design, unpublished document prepared for the Environment Agency

O'Connor, T P, 1982 *Animal bones from Flaxengate, Lincoln, c. 870–1500*, The archaeology of Lincoln **18/1**, London

Peake, H, 1931 *The archaeology of Berkshire*, London

Pearce, J and Vince, A, 1988 *A dated type-series of London medieval pottery. Part 4: Surrey White-wares*, London Middlesex Archaeol Soc special pap **10**, [London]

Pike, G, 1965 A medieval pottery kiln site on the Camley Gardens Estate, Maidenhead, *Berkshire Archaeol J* **62**, 22–33

Poulton, R, 1978 Cropmarks at Stanwell, near Heathrow Airport, *London Archaeol* **39**, 239–42

Powell, A J and Clark, K C, 1996 Exploitation of domestic animals in the Iron Age at Rooksdown, unpublished report prepared for the Centre for Human Ecology and Environment, Southampton University

Redknap, M, 1991 The Saxon pottery from Barking Abbey: part 1, local wares; part 2, the continental imports, *London Archaeol* **6/13**, 353–60; **6/14**, 378–81

Reed, M, 1979 The Buckinghamshire landscape, in *The making of the English landscape* (eds W G Hoskins and R Millward), London

Richards, J D, 1999 What's so special about 'productive' sites? Middle Saxon settlements in Northumbria, in *The making of kingdoms* (eds T Dickinson and D Griffiths), Anglo-Saxon Stud Archaeol and Hist **10**, Oxford Univ Committee Archaeol, 71–80, Oxford

Riddler, I D, Trzaska-Nartowski, N I A and Hatton, S, forthcoming, in Early medieval craft. Objects and waste of bone, antler and ivory

from Ipswich Excavations, 1974–1994, London

Robinson, M A, 1988 Molluscan evidence for pasture and meadowland on the floodplain of the Upper Thames basin, in *The exploitation of wetlands* (eds P Murphy and C French), 101–12, BAR (Brit Ser) **186**, Oxford

Robinson, M A, 1992 Environment, archaeology and alluvium on the river gravels of the South Midlands, in *Alluvial archaeology in Britain* (eds S P Needham and M G Macklin), Oxbow Monogr **27**, 197–208, Oxford

Robinson, M A and Lambrick, G H 1984 Holocene alluviation and hydrology in the Upper Thames basin, *Nature* (London) **308**, 809–14

Rocque J, 1761 *A topographical map of the County of Berks*, [London]

Roden, D, 1969 Enclosure in the Chiltern Hills, *Geographical Annals* **51–2**, 115–26

Rogers, N S H, 1993 Anglian and other finds from Fishergate, *The Archaeology of York*, **17/9**, London

Rutland, R A, and Greenaway, J A, 1969 Archaeological notes from Reading Museum, *Berkshire Archaeol J* **64**, 39

Rutland, R A and Greenaway, J A, 1970 Archaeological notes from Reading Museum *Berkshire Archaeol J* **65**, 57

Sadler, P, 1990 Faunal remains, in *Faccombe Netherton. Excavation of a Saxon and medieval manorialcComplex I* (J N Fairbrother), British Museum Occas Pap **74**, 462–506, London

Sawyer, P H, 1968 *Anglo-Saxon charters, an annotated list and bibliography*, Roy Hist Soc, London

Scheuer, J L, Musgrave, J H and Evans, S P, 1980 The estimation of late foetal and perinatal age from limb bone length by linear and logarithmic regression, *Annals of human biology* **7 (3)**, 257–65

Schwarz-Mackensen, G, 1976 *Die Knochennadeln von Haithabu, Berichte uber die Ausgrabungen in Haithabu* **9**, Neumunster

Sherlock, R L, 1947 British regional geology, *London and Thames Valley*, 2nd edn, HMSO London

Short, B, 1989 The geography of England and Wales in 1910: an evaluation of Lloyd George's 'Domesday' of land ownership, *Historical Geography Res Ser* **22**

Sparey-Green, C, 1984 Early Anglo-Saxon burials from the Trumpet Major, Allington Avenue, *Proc Dorset Natur Hist Archaeol Soc*, **106**, 149–52

Stanley, C, 1972 Bray Roman cemetery, Berkshire, *CBA Group 9 Newsletter* **2**, 12

Stenton, F M, 1913 *The early history of the Abbey of Abingdon*, Oxford

Stephanus, Eddius 1927 *Life of Bishop Wilfrid* (text, trans. and notes by B Colgrave), Cambridge

Stephens, J, 1884 On the remains found in an Anglo-Saxon tumulus at Taplow, Bucks, *J Brit Archaeol Ass* **40**, 61–71

Stocker, D and Went, D, with an introduction by Farley, M, 1995 The evidence for a pre-Viking church adjacent to the Anglo-Saxon barrow at Taplow, Buckinghamshire, *Archaeol J* **152,** 441–54

Tate, W E, 1978 *A Domesday of English enclosure acts and awards*, University of Reading

Timby, J, 1988 The Middle Saxon pottery, in *Southampton finds volume one: the coins and pottery from Hamwic* (ed. P Andrews), Southampton Archaeol Monogr **4**, 73–121, [Southampton]

Timby, J R, 1996 *The Anglo-Saxon cemetery at Empingham II, Rutland*, Oxbow Monogr **70**, Oxford

Trow-Smith, R, 1957 *English husbandry from the earliest times to the present day*, London

Ulmschneider, K, 2000 Settlement, economy and the 'productive' site: Middle Anglo-Saxon Lincolnshire AD 650–780, *Medieval Archaeol* **44**, 53–79

Underwood, R, 1998 *Anglo-Saxon weapons and warfare*, Oxford

VCH 1925, *Victoria History of the County of Buckinghamshire* **3**, London

Wade-Martins, P, 1980 Excavations in North Elmham Park 1967–1972, *EAA* **9**, Gressenhall

Walton Rogers, P, 1997 Textile production at 16–22 Coppergate: the small finds, *The Archaeology of York* **17/11**, London

Waterman, D M, 1959 Late Saxon, Viking and Early Medieval Finds from York, *Archaeologia* **97**, 59–105

Webster, L E, and Cherry, J, 1979 Medieval Britain, *Medieval Archaeol* **24**, 233

Webster, L E, and Cherry, J, 1980 Warwickshire, Bidford-on-Avon, Medieval Britain in 1979, *Medieval Archaeology* **24**, 233

West, S E, 1985 West Stow: the Anglo-Saxon village, vol 1, *EAA*, **24**, Gressenhall

West, B, 1988 Birds and mammals, in Two Middle Saxon occupation sites at Jubilee Hall and 21–22 Maiden Lane (R Cowie and R L Whytehead), *Trans London Middlesex Archaeol Soc* **39**, 150–4

West, B, 1989 Animal remains: material hand-collected, in Excavations at the Peabody site, Chandos Place and the National Gallery (RL Whytehead and R Cowie), *Trans London Middlesex Archaeol Soc* **40**, 150–67

Whitelock, D, 1961 *The Anglo-Saxon Chronicle. A revised translation*, London

Whittingham, L S, 1997 Pottery assessment for Church Farm, Bierton, Buckinghamshire, OAU unpublished report

Whytehead, R L, Cowie R, and Blackmore L, 1989 Excavations at the Peabody Site, Chandos Place and the National Gallery, *Trans London Middlesex Archaeol Soc* **40**, 35–176

Wilson, D R, 1972 Roman Britain in 1971, *Britannia* **3**, 299–367

Wilson, D, 1992 *Anglo-Saxon Paganism*, London

Wilson, D M, and Hurst, J G, 1958 Medieval Britain in 1957: Old Windsor, *Medieval Archaeol* **2**, 183–5

Wymer, J, 1959 Archaeological notes *Berkshire Archaeol J* **57**, 124

Young, F A, 1979 *Guide to the Local Administrative Units of England, Vol 1: Southern England*, Roy Hist Soc, London

Yorke, B, 1995, *Wessex in the Early Middle Ages*, Leicester

Yule, B, 1988 Natural topography of north Southwark, in *Excavations in Southwark, 1973–1976; Lambeth 1973–1979*, Museum of London Department of Greater London Archaeology, LAMAS/SAS Joint Publication, **3**, 13–18

INDEX

Illustrations are denoted by page numbers in *italics* or by *illus* where figures are scattered throughout the text.